High Value Consulting

High Value Consulting

Managing and Maximizing
External and Internal
Consultants
For Massive Added Value

Tom Lambert

NICHOLAS BREALEY
PUBLISHING
LONDON

First published by
Nicholas Brealey Publishing Limited in 1998

36 John Street	671 Clover Drive
London	Santa Rosa
WC1A 2AT, UK	CA 95401, USA
Tel: +44 (0)171 430 0224	Tel: (707) 566 8006
Fax: +44 (0)171 404 8311	*Fax: (707) 566 8005*

http://www.nbrealey-books.com

© Tom Lambert 1998

The right of Tom Lambert to be identified as the author of this work has been asserted in accordance with the Copyright, Designs and Patents Act 1988.

ISBN 1-85788-173-7

British Library Cataloguing in Publication Data
A catalogue record for this book is available from the British Library.

All rights reserved. No part of this publication may be reproduced, stored in a retrieval system, or transmitted, in any form or by any means, electronic, mechanical, photocopying, recording and/or otherwise without the prior written permission of the publishers. This book may not be lent, resold, hired out or otherwise disposed of by way of trade in any form, binding or cover other than that in which it is published, without the prior consent of the publishers.

Printed in Finland by Werner Söderström Oy.

Also by Tom Lambert:

The Power of Influence:
Intensive Influencing Skills at Work
Published by Nicholas Brealey, 1996

Key Management Solutions
Published by Pitman, 1996

High Income Consulting:
How to Build and Market Your Professional Practice
Published by Nicholas Brealey, 2nd edn 1997

Making Change Pay
Published by Financial Times, 1997

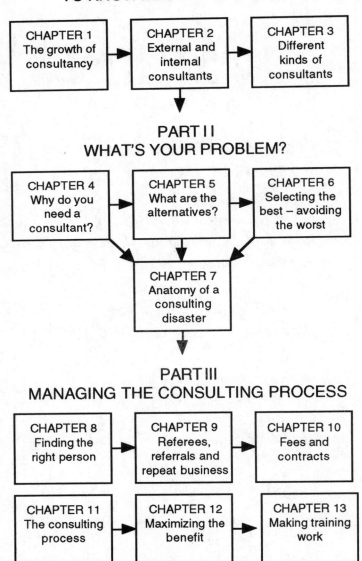

Contents

Foreword ix

Part I Everything You Always Wanted to Know about Consulting 1
1   The growth of consultancy 3
2   External and internal consultants 13
3   Different kinds of consultants 23

Part II What's Your Problem? 45
4   Why do you need a consultant? 47
5   What are the alternatives? 63
6   Selecting the best – avoiding the worst 69
7   Anatomy of a consulting disaster 79

Part III Managing the Consulting Process 95
8   Finding the right person 97
9   Referees, referrals and repeat business 115
10 Fees and contracts 125
11 The consulting process 147
12 Maximizing the benefit 165
13 Making training work 187

Afterword 199
Bibliography 201
Index 207

Foreword

THOSE WHO WRITE BOOKS OUGHT TO POSSESS A STEELY CORE OF unmitigated arrogance. After all, we have no choice but to assume that we have something worth saying and that large numbers of people will want to read our pontifications.

I have written what many people have kindly called the most useful book about the field of consultancy, *High Income Consulting*, and as a result have been called 'the consultant's consultant' by the quality press. Putting this another way, I am deemed by others to know a little more about consultancy than most. My *Key Management Solutions* began life as a detailed 'how to do it' collection on the consultancy process.

I have not always been on my present side of the fence. I have been a client and have had direct experience with a major conglomerate choosing, using and sometimes firing consultants.

And as a working consultant I have helped clients do a range of important things:

❑ develop practical dominance strategies and make them work
❑ raise essential capital in one hectic day when a successful bid for a major contract threatened the cashflow of an underresourced but technologically supreme client
❑ kickstart failed initiatives from total quality to change programs
❑ triple sales and profits by helping make sales training work.

So although I have sat on both sides, I have done so without being tempted to nail my colors to the mast. I have an ax to grind, but I sharpen it to cut down ineffectiveness on both sides. I think that this qualifies me to throw a small light on both management and consultancy to the potential benefit of both.

Chapter 7 looks at what happens when consultancy goes badly wrong, but also tries to identify how the disaster, which in business terms is the near equivalent of the sinking of the *Titanic*, might have been avoided. Too often the differences in expectation between the client and the consultant are such that problems and, worse, ultimate failure to achieve the promised benefits become inevitable. Consultancy is both too important and too expensive to allow it to fail.

As I hope this book will make plain, the benefits which can come from effective use of consultants either from outside or within your organization can be immense. The right consultant, properly managed, can make your firm many times what you spend on their services. And in a rapidly changing business environment you will almost certainly need to hire a consultant at some time – if you don't get it right first time, you may not be around to try it again.

The only way to be confident of tapping into the enormous added value which is available is to manage selection and control. To do this managers must be able to read between the lines of consultant speak. This is only possible if you know the business and it is sometimes difficult even then without a resource or a reminder.

Costs must also be controlled. Anything done in a business should be done to the highest possible standards at the lowest possible price. Trying to do consultancy on the cheap, however, is likely to lead to considerable waste and no worthwhile outcomes. Like any commodity or service consultancy should be bought on the basis of value rather then price.

Foreword

A consultancy intervention should be an unique growth opportunity for all involved. When a consultant leaves the client premises for the last time, the client and the management team should be more capable of dealing with future uncertainties as well as today's emerging needs.

Look where you will in the world, consultancy brings great benefits or it creates great mischief. It seldom follows a middle road, but if client and consultant learn to work together effectively, massive added value will come about almost as a matter of course. This book is, if you will, a manual for working together. I am not seeking to stamp a 'government health warning' on consultants. I know, and my clients know, what we can achieve if we work effectively together. Writing this book has given me the opportunity to examine my beliefs and, although I think the whole cloth has stood up well to the examination, I have been forced to make a small darn here and there. This is as it should be. Part of the added value of having clients and consultants working effectively together is that it accelerates the growth of both.

I hope this book will be read, and more importantly used, by clients and consultants alike. Clients will continue to spend more and more on hiring consultants. Long-term survival and short- and long-term prosperity will demand inputs from beyond the organization. Consultants, in their turn, must be ready to provide otherwise unreachable added value. We can do it, but only if we are ready to dose ourselves with the same medicines we prescribe to others.

We must swallow our pride and take our medicine because we are, increasingly, not the only game in town. A growing number of organizations ranging from computer companies to the Royal Air Force have learned the value of internal consultancy teams. I have helped clients create and develop such teams and the experience has shown me that the ideal is to use internal and external resources in tandem for greatest economy, autonomy and growth.

I don't expect this book to make me popular in some quarters. My day job is to give frank, timely and unbiased advice and if I occasionally tread on the odd oversensitive toe, please accept that I do so believing passionately in the value of that job.

Tom Lambert
Wheathampstead, Hertfordshire, UK
and Barrington, Illinois, USA

Author's note
Rather than continually repeating 'his or her', I have opted to make the client 'him' and the consultant 'her' throughout the book.

Part I

Everything You Always Wanted to Know About Consulting

1
The Growth of Consultancy

The second oldest profession, that of giving, or rather selling, advice.

Howard Shenson

THIS BOOK IS WRITTEN FOR BOTH USERS OF CONSULTANCY AND consultants themselves. It will enable users of consultancy to get optimal service at reasonable cost. Consultants will, I hope, give what they read considerable thought and, by turning thought into appropriate action, will enhance the reputation and protect the future of their profession.

My belief is that, at a minimum, professional consultants must:

- play a significant part in enabling our client to exploit a legitimate business opportunity or solve a complex problem
- meet or exceed predetermined, quantifiable business goals

- satisfy our client and any qualified third party that we have added value in the form of meaningful non-measurable outcomes
- accelerate the development of the client's people and/or organization
- enhance the client organization's autonomy
- avoid drawing out the assignment beyond the legitimate needs of the brief
- avoid any possible conflict of interest
- charge professionally established and fully justifiable fees.

Where are we now?

The consultancy business is growing as never before. More and different types of organizations are turning to consultants for help. A recent report published in the US even suggested that there is a shortage of consultants and yet there are obvious signs of consultant fatigue both in the media and in the minds of business decision makers. What lies behind this paradox?

Organizations need more consultancy help for a number of reasons. Technology is advancing rapidly and it is virtually impossible for the working manager to keep up to date without external help. Global best practice is becoming less an option and more a necessity and the knowledge required most often lies outside the organization. Business is increasingly a zero-sum game in which new ideas are needed to shorten the sales process as well as to get new products and services first to market: this demands new approaches that tend to come from outside.

Privatization, pseudo-privatization and environmental protection do not necessarily go together, but they all require experts to make them viable. All of these are good reasons for seeking and using outside help, but there are less valid reasons for the growth of consultancy.

Managers are still fad junkies. Research by leading consultancy Bain and Co shows that Japanese, French, US and British managers run each other close in their anxiety to incorporate the latest fallacies and futilities of impractical management thinking into their businesses. This is good for consultancy revenues, but whether it is good for the client companies is open to the severest questioning. At best a high percentage of such initiatives fail to deliver the promised benefits. At worst, they damage morale, increase the resistance to change within the workforce and make necessary change more difficult, more expensive and less likely to succeed.

Business is by no means the only source of a difficult to justify, massive growth in consultancy earnings. Government has gone in for consultancy in a big way and by no means always in furtherance of public wellbeing. Too often governments have used consultants to rubber stamp executive decisions that have already been taken or to be able to blame them for unpopular measures. One report, by the UK National Audit Commission, suggested that the improvements brought about by government expenditure on consultancy were equal to approximately 10 percent of the spend.

Nobody loves us

The consultancy business has become rather like prostitution: not only is there very little that we are not prepared to do for cash but, as an industry, our relationship with our clients is in danger of becoming one of mutual distaste.

In spite of the proliferation of 'one-man bands', consultancy is still dominated by the big firms. And the big firms are getting bigger. Let us look briefly at why some who have bought their services are less than enchanted with their work.

The top consultancy companies have a great many partners. These are experienced and knowledgeable people who would be a major asset to any corporation. They demand, and are entitled to, high earnings; many of them enjoy more than $1 million a year in addition to the increasing value of their share of a growing and successful business. They are *la crème de la crème*, but there is a small problem.

Suppose that there are 235 working days available each year which can be billed (that is 365 days less 104 Saturdays and Sundays, plus an average of 6 public holidays and, say, 20 days' annual vacation). If I am to make an income of $1 million I need to charge a minimum of $4255 a day, every day. The price may be acceptable but the working schedule is impossible. It would leave no time for self-development, managerial responsibilities, marketing or selling. If I fell down on any of these, I would quickly fail to find work and my seven-figure income would be in jeopardy.

What I need to do is to grow some 'green beans'. Green beans are the multiplying factor which will enable my income to grow while I spend my time in leisurely, or frenetic, pursuit of ever more business. Green beans are young, inexperienced, well-qualified, usually ill-trained graduates who can be used at the client's premises to do the actual work. Under the umbrella of a top consultancy name they can be charged out at a rate far in excess of their salary and can provide, between them, much of my remuneration and that of my equally highly paid co-partners. *The Economist* has estimated the revenues generated by an average McKinsey employee at $469,000 a year in 1995. Beans have not created such dramatic results since Jack traded his cow for a handful of them. What is more, the sometimes minimal training that inexperienced consultants are given before being set free in the client's premises can be sales training and they can be told that their first responsibility is to look for the next assignment.

The only fly in my sweet smelling unguent is the client. When he agreed to what he thought was a very high price, he thought he was buying an experienced consultant's personal services. However bright the green beans are, they are not the principal and clients are not fickle creatures to be won over with brightness, youth and charm. If they believe they have bought age, experience and wisdom, they feel a little cheated if they don't get it.

So consultant fatigue comes from expecting one thing and experiencing another, but it doesn't end there. Fairly or unfairly, some clients mistrust the close, some would say too close, relationship between the audit and accountancy operations of the major firms and their consultant colleagues.

The professional accountancy bodies have made their position clear: the accountancy and audit function must not be used to tout for consultancy business. 'Chinese walls' must be constructed and remain intact. But ex-partners of what used to be thought of as the 'Big Six' can still be heard talking of the high percentage of the marketing budget which was spent on entertaining their audit and accountancy brethren. And sadly one still meets the occasional client who believes that they were once talked by an auditor into accepting consultancy 'help'. True or false, a little mud sticks and mires the reputation of two professions.

However, never let it be thought that the less than desirable reputation of consultants results only from the activities of the big players. The recession of the early 1990s led to unprecedented levels of white-collar redundancies. The consultancy profession on both sides of the Atlantic has been swelled by large numbers of self-employed one-person bands or small partnerships. Like green beans at the other end of the age divide, many if not most of these people are intelligent, hard-working and, within limits, capable. Unhappily, however, some lack even the most basic skills of advising organizations. They do not have process skills and their advice is often limited to recommending what they did so successfully in companies such as IBM or GM in the 1970s. Worse, some with a cynical disregard for the principles and practices of marketing stretch the truth when listing their qualifications.

I remember once meeting an 'ex-managing director' whose actual previous experience was the ownership of a shop which had unfortunately gone bankrupt. I am sure she was not actually telling a lie – no doubt the shop was a limited company – but her interpretation of 'managing director' would not be shared by the client. In a profession dependent on trust, such situations, multiplied many times, tend to worry the punters.

I have been asked by self-styled strategic consultants if I would explain to them what a mission statement is and how to conduct a SWOT analysis. And I have received too many calls along the lines of the following:

- Is that Tom Lambert?
- Yes.
- Good, I want you to do something for me.
- How can I help?
- I'm a consultant and I've landed a job doing a business plan for a client.
- Excellent. Congratulations. But I don't quite see...
- What I want you to do is to write me a step-by-step guide to producing a business plan.
- Why would you want that?
- Well, I've never done one before, have I?

Too often, small consultancies are under-resourced in knowledge as well as in the tools of the trade and occasionally individuals exaggerate their experience to get business. Both are likely to be to the detriment of the client. Unfortunately the good, of whom there are many, become tarnished with the misdeeds of the bad and the general reputation of the profession suffers.

Brave new world

So we have a paradox in which as the need for consultancy grows faith in the profession declines. The consultancy business has grown, is growing and there is no reason why it ought to be diminishing. In a period of intense change the wise individual seeks knowledge wherever it may be found.

Change is the mother of consultancy and information is the father. While change continues to accelerate and information, or better knowledge, is perceived as the essential competitive edge, consultancy sales will grow at a rate that breeding rabbits ought to envy.

Such growth means that less than qualified individuals will be drawn to consultancy, companies will be tempted to cut corners as never before and the use of green beans will proliferate. *Caveat emptor* is no longer enough. Clients need to be given high-quality, basic, everyday tools that will:

- ❏ enable them to determine when to use consultants and when to do the job themselves
- ❏ ensure that, when consultants are used, the organization gains the greatest possible return on their outlay, including accelerated development of employees and greater

problem-solving and opportunity-exploiting autonomy for the future
- an enhanced ability to think strategically, including thinking about how they will leverage the commercial potential of what they learn about consultancy in the process of using consulting assistance.

But clients also need to realize that if they are uncertain about the value of the consultancy advice they receive, much of the fault may lie with themselves.

Clients rarely think their problems through to the extent of being able to specify the outcomes that would make the expenditure worthwhile. They all too often hide behind vagueness, only a small amount of which is justified, and try, sometimes by a variety of creative means, to avoid the difficult business of independent thought. Thus when the job has been done there is an indistinct feeling that whether the outcome is poor, mediocre or brilliant, it could have been better.

Another problem with clients is that they read and are seduced by the latest business bestseller. This may tell them what to do, but it rarely tells them how to do it.

So they hire consultants to give an injection of the most heavily hyped panacea, even though it may not be relevant to their business. Whether it is the 'let my people go' school of empowerment or the 'shape the job until it ceases to be their job' school of business process reengineering, the initiative is likely to fail.

Not a zero-sum game

In this book I propose to provide consultant and client alike with the basic tools and ideas that will enable both to gain the most from the client–consultant relationship.

Consulting is not a zero-sum game. The more you win the more I win and, in an increasingly competitive world, we need each other to be consistent winners.

2
External and Internal Consultants

If our people develop faster than competitors' people, then they are worth more.

James M. Biggar

As we will see in Part II, it is not always necessary to use an external consultant. In some circumstances you may have a person or a team within your organization that has the skills and knowledge to do the work you require; sometimes an external perspective is invaluable, whatever your own staff's abilities. Both external and internal consultants have their advantages and disadvantages.

The effective consultant, whether internal or external:

❑ listens to understand rather than to judge, at least initially
❑ asks careful supplementary questions to add to their understanding

- works flexibly and with commitment to ensure that pre-determined outcomes are achieved in time at minimum cost
- analyses problems and opportunities and, better, helps those directly involved to see and evaluate new alternatives
- helps to push strategic and creative thinking down through the organization
- opens and keeps open effective channels of communication
- helps to change the culture of the organization from blame fixing to problem solving and opportunity grasping.

Doing it yourself

Many organizations that would deny they have internal consultants have been using them successfully for years.

- If you changed the shape of your organization to a matrix any time within the last 20 years
- if you depend on a human resource department to advise on anything from salaries to social policy
- if you put together project groups for special assignments; if you rely on your own information systems specialists to ensure the most effective use of computers
- if you have strategic or learning alliances with other companies whereby your people and theirs share ideas and experiences to avoid repeating mistakes and to save money
- if you use trainers to facilitate meetings and introduce new time-saving ideas such as metaplanning or ideas hypermarkets
- if indeed you have an internal training department at all

then you have an internal consultancy capacity.

External and Internal Consultants

There are real advantages, if you hire an external consultant, in letting some of your brightest and best work alongside her, for at least part of the time. Your staff will accelerate their learning, understand far more of the intervention strategy and become champions for making it work in the real business world – and they will do work that would normally cost you a fat daily fee. You also get your desired results more quickly, as the consultant is able to concentrate on more complex activities which need her special skills.

If you have an internal consultancy team you enjoy all these advantages plus one – you no longer have to pay expensive fees to an outsider except where the need is highly specialized or you decide that you can make better use of your internal people's time. So having an internal consultancy capacity gives you greater economy, greater flexibility and enhanced development of your better people.

Specific advantages

Internal consultants enjoy a couple of great advantages over outsiders. First, they understand the culture of the business from the inside. Of course, there is a constant danger that they may be prisoners of that culture, but this can be avoided if they are recognized and treated as what they are, the instruments of change.

Innumerable politicians in recent years have talked about 'thinking the unthinkable'. Edward de Bono has argued that all businesses ought to have, recognize and revere a licensed jester, someone who is able to think and say the unthinkable. Organizations need a team of experienced and able people charged with a responsibility to think well beyond the confines of the box.

Secondly, unlike the external consultant who moves on when her job is finished, the internal consultant remains to see good made better and better made superlative as people pick up and run with the ball that has been passed to them.

Someone who has truly learned to do something new applies their creative skills and new-found confidence to initiate more and more exciting and profitable activities. Costs are reduced again and again as finding better ways of doing things and increasing productivity becomes the norm.

Quality standards get better and better at lower cost until the organization becomes the model of its industry and then begins to shape its sector's future. Profits increase as more and more profitable customers are enticed away from competition and all stakeholders share in the value created.

Job satisfaction and security increase and go on increasing as strategic thinking is pushed down to every level of the business and emerging customer desires are consistently exceeded.

And few people want to leave an organization in which people's creativity and commitment have been released in this way. Unlike the external consultant, the internal team can watch their work continue to flower over many years.

Personal satisfaction

From a purely personal viewpoint there are further reasons for individuals wanting to make the effort to act as internal consultants.

You can expect a wide range of interesting assignments. My first real job, after being a graduate recruit in training, was as a district marketing manager for General Motors. I was expected to ensure that my twenty or so dealerships achieved their sales, profit and, most importantly, their purchasing tar-

External and Internal Consultants

gets by using something known as the 'pull-through' effect. This was a concept that went something like this:

- the relationship between GM and its dealers was considered to be a special one, much closer than that of vendor and customer
- it would be inappropriate in such a situation to sell to the dealer
- but GM wanted to grow its business
- so district marketing managers worked to improve their dealers' business
- and dealers, having sold more, bought more without any indecent pressure being applied.

So I, fresh out of college and wet behind the ears, had to find ways to understand all the operations of a business and deliver advice to someone who had probably run the operation since before I was born. Just as I loved it so will you, young or old. The person who is not motivated by doing something different with different and interesting people almost every day is dull indeed.

You will also experience accelerated personal development. You will be forced to learn, and learn fast, how your particular business and industry generally work and how to get your most 'off the wall' ideas across to hard-bitten professionals in such a way that they will follow your advice and prosper.

You will learn to influence behavior. Internal consultants are usually people with a mission. They know that their ideas are worthwhile and they thirst to see them used. When I had the opportunity in GM, I ensured that all executives above a certain level learned state-of-the-art sales skills. In this way I could be sure that those who had great ideas could get them across to their peers, subordinates and superiors effectively. It is still my preferred way – hence *The Power of Influence* – but whether you learn through training, self-development or experience, your skills will be of immense value all your working life both to you and to your employers.

As you demonstrate your ability people will want to challenge you further, by offering bigger and better assignments or fast-track promotion. As others challenge you, you will challenge yourself. You will spend your life in an accelerating upward spiral of personal improvement and you will love the journey.

You will consistently develop win–win relationships. Departmental parochialism, internecine strife, hidden agendas and infighting too often replace cooperation in today's organizations. You will have the opportunity to educate and manage decision makers so that the focus is on beating the real enemy, those other companies who aim to take your most profitable customers and with them your corporate and personal prosperity. By example, by precept, by the application of your skills and, if necessary, by the authority represented by your superior knowledge, you will have the opportunity to make a real difference and to redirect the macho spirit to where it will do most good.

You will experience more productive use of your time. You will learn the truth of the saying that you learn more with your mouth shut and your ears open than you do with mouth open and ears shut. Importantly, you will learn that through something as simple as effective listening you can actually raise the energy of those around to a degree where the excitement and commitment become contagious. So you will learn to spend better than 60 percent of your time listening and learning. When you are not listening you will be indulging in an activity which none of us can resist: giving advice. What could be a more productive or fascinating use of your time?

Where will they come from?

Successful internal consultants can come from anywhere in the organization. Internal consultants I have helped train have included:

- an internal auditor who, in spite of his professional background, held a strong and legitimate view that he was really a 'people person'
- a marketeer involved in the recognition of changing customer desires and the development of new products
- management development specialists who wanted opportunities to apply their theories and models to the real world
- computer and information systems specialists who wanted the chance to help people get the most out of the corporation's investment in technology
- industrial relations specialists who were tired of confrontation and, from the other side of that particular fence, at least one union leader
- corporate lawyers
- a production superintendent who had a burning desire to help expand people's ability to work within the greater team rather than remaining members of a narrow parochial group intent on defending their own turf
- public relations specialists
- other people as diverse as scientists, engineers, accountants and factory foremen.

Look for people in your organization who show evidence of the characteristics in the checklist on page 20.

- ✔ They think before they speak, but not for too long.
- ✔ They are comfortable with their education and show some evidence of an ability and a desire to learn.
- ✔ They enjoy helping others, but not as an excuse to escape from the tedium of what they ought to be doing.
- ✔ They are disciplined yet flexible in their approach to work.
- ✔ They demonstrate a sensitivity in reading and responding to group behavior.
- ✔ They are able to separate personal issues from work issues and, remaining sensitive to both, are still able to get what must be done accomplished to time.
- ✔ They are effective listeners.
- ✔ They appreciate the impact of their behavior on others and are able to adapt to the needs of the situation.
- ✔ They can deal with conflict and anger and will confront, rather than step away from, conflict without taking perverse pleasure in creating it.
- ✔ They understand the key difference between empathy, 'you have the right to feel as you do', and sympathy, 'you are right to feel as you do', and practice the former.
- ✔ They can build an atmosphere of trust and openness even where mistrust and anger are driving others.
- ✔ They are able to cut through a plethora of confusion to identify the essential facts and are able to recognize that people's feelings are facts in any situation.
- ✔ They are self-reliant, but will ask others for help rather than risk getting it wrong.
- ✔ They sell their ideas effectively and rarely blame others for failing to understand.
- ✔ They contribute a range of proven techniques and models to facilitate progress in discussions.
- ✔ They evaluate ideas critically and effectively but avoid the copout of claiming to be the 'devil's advocate'.

This appears to be a great deal to ask of people. It is meant to be. The internal consultant, like her external counterpart, must be effective in a wide range of situations with a wider range of unique individuals. The list, though comprehensive, is by no means exhaustive. Indeed, you would be well advised to regard it as a list of basic requirements to which you will add rather than a demand for paragons which you will trim to fit the realities of your situation.

If you are going to the trouble and expense of putting together and training internal consultants, you owe it to yourself to maximize the probability of their success. This means in practice that you demand the highest standards in everything from the beginning. All that you would expect from an external consultant you should demand from any that you appoint internally.

One last thought: an internal consultancy capability can accelerate and enhance the future of the company, but for some it has done much more. Some world-beating corporations with internal consultancy teams have taken the idea further. Having built and proved the competence of their consultants in their own operations, they now sell their skills to non-competitive businesses. Thus they create new revenue streams that benefit from rapidly expanding world demand and, at the same time, they bring a flow of new ideas from many industries into the core business.

3

Different Kinds of Consultants

You must be part Sherlock Holmes, part Sigmund Freud.
Victor Kiam

IN THE PREVIOUS CHAPTER WE DISCUSSED THE CHARACTERISTICS and advantages of internal consultants. This chapter will consider the various kinds of special consultants that you are likely to encounter and the differences between big and small consultancies.

Individuals within the consultancy profession fall broadly into two groupings, operational and advisory, each of which has a further subdivision, process and functional.

Operational consultants

These are the people who are prepared to roll up their sleeves and help get the job done. Indeed, they will often do the whole job from start to finish. Each is an extra pair of, hopefully expert, hands. They might be market researchers or tacticians, world-class manufacturing gurus, trainers, project management consultants, company doctors or interim managers, or they may be in any one of a hundred disciplines.

The important thing about them is their willingness to become involved. Frequently small companies have little choice other than to use operational consultants – where human resources are limited, nothing may be done unless the consultant buckles down to do at least some of it.

Because they get involved at the coal face, operational consultants tend to enjoy somewhat longer assignments than some of their colleagues. This is to their benefit as they need to take up less of their productive time looking for work. From the client viewpoint it also means that the daily fee rate is likely to be somewhat lower. Unfortunately for the consultant, even a relatively low fee may seem high from the perspective of the client.

For example, the CEO of a small to medium company earning, say, $150,000 a year may, in an idle moment, have worked out that for 261 days (365 less 52 weekends) he earns $574.71 a day. Given that the consultant is assigned to doing a task under his direction and is, in effect, a temporary employee, a modest daily rate of $1000 may appear to be verging on the exorbitant.

This is a misunderstanding, of course. The CEO is paid for 261 days whether he works, enjoys a day on the golf course or relaxes on the beach during his annual vacation. The consultant, operational or otherwise, is only paid when she is directly serving the client. What she is paid must provide her with annual earnings which reflect her worth in the marketplace. If reality dictates that she can only work for a client on 150 days a year and if she, like her client, is worth $150,000 a year in the job market, she is in trouble if she charges $1000 a day. That is enough to cover her salary, but it takes no account of the cost of running her business. Take her overheads out of the equation and she is actually earning considerably less than her client.

Advisory consultants

In an ideal world all of us would be advisory consultants. Those of us who are able to go into a client's premises, look around for a while and make a pronouncement that will make us a very comfortable income while being worth millions to our delighted clients are to be envied. Tom Peters, when he is not conducting workshops, or Sir John Harvey-Jones would fall into this category, as would Faith Popcorn.

It is not that these luminaries don't work – far from it, they work extremely hard – but much of the tough labor takes place far away from the view of any client. When they are at the client corporation they dazzle with the apparent ease with which are able to cut through the clutter and give immense added value in a few words.

I had and, to a degree, still have a healthy skepticism with respect to the big name business gurus. However, I also have a client who a while ago hired Tom Peters to spend a day working with his board of directors. When he saw what Peters quoted for what was assumed to be a single day's work my client was almost taken physically ill, but a deal is a deal.

So what did he get for his money? First the Peters team researched his industry, nationally and globally. Then they researched his company's actual and potential standing in that industry both inside and outside the company. By the time Tom Peters met with the board I am told that he was able to give analysis and advice which it would have taken all of the company's resources months to put together. Multiply the salaries of a team of busy executives and directors by even a couple of months, throw in the cost of failing to do what they otherwise should have been doing and then compare this with the cost of a day spent in the company of a uniquely well-informed and far-sighted business guru and you have an idea, perhaps, of why my client believes that the prince's ransom he spent ranks high among the best investments he ever made.

So we have a division between the doers and the advisers – operational and advisory consultants – that is useful although far from precise. You would not expect Faith Popcorn to sit and write your marketing plan or Sir John Harvey-Jones to shift a machine which is causing a bottleneck in your manufacturing plant – and of course advisory consultancy is not limited to the world famous. I, in my relatively modest way, am an advisory consultant who, like some of my more distinguished peers, also gets my hands a little dirty from time to time.

So, before you go too far, you must be clear: do you want the use of a highly specialized and very expensive brain or do you need a more modest brain combined with a willing pair of hands? Having decided that, you may next want to consider whether you need process or more functional skills.

Process consultants

Process consultants are a little like caddies at a golf tournament. We carry in our minds a comprehensive range of clubs and we have specialized knowledge of the courses and their difficulties so we can advise meaningfully on what wood or iron to use in almost any circumstance. If you want to know how to downsize without encountering either Auschwitz or Altzheimer's we can provide you with the tools; and when problems or unforeseen opportunities emerge we have other techniques that will deal with the changing circumstances. We can give you game plans that will improve your leadership style or deliver problem-solving techniques precisely attuned to the difficulty you need to overcome.

We try hard not to become embroiled in content. Our world is the world of ideas, concepts and models. In addition, if we are any good, we can tell you much of what the research says about your situation, the degree to which it can be trusted and how to adapt its findings to your needs. We can show you how others have used the tools we advocate and explain precisely the circumstances in which each will be most effective.

Our toolkit is appropriate to all managers in every kind of organization. Although we prefer to see you apply our tools and own the outcomes, we provide added value by sharing our experience of other organizations and other countries. We are usually advisory consultants, but our enthusiasm often causes us to roll up our sleeves. If you require a toolkit precisely attuned to your changing needs, you need a process consultant.

Functional consultants

There are two types of functional consultant: the industry specialist and the role expert. The industry specialist may know all there is to know about the automotive trade, textiles, banking or whatever. The specialism may be narrow – forecourt petrol sales – or broad – the finance sector. It may be a part of a sector – heavy commercial vehicles or parts and accessories – or it may be anything to do with transport – air, road, rail or water. No matter how deep or broad the knowledge you need you will find it, but to find it you must understand what you want.

We all have a natural tendency to assume that our circumstances are unique. The need for a very narrow specialism is often grossly over-rated. The differences between yellow widgets and blue widgets may, for all I know, be real, but for all practical purposes I am prepared to bet that the consultant whose background is in the making and selling of green widgets will be able to serve in either industry to everyone's satisfaction if given a chance. I, for example, started my consultancy career as an automotive specialist. I have subsequently delighted clients in industries as diverse as banking and cattle ranching.

Narrow specialisms undoubtedly have their place, but that kind of specialist knowledge is required far less often than its proponents would have us believe. Indeed, there is a major downside to too narrow a specialism. To have developed such a restricted area of expertise the specialist may well have spent almost all of their working life with or in a very small number of companies. There is little chance of him possessing a wider perspective on your particular problems and opportunities.

There *are* functional consultants who revel in industrial diversity, nevertheless. Those who specialize in, for example, marketing, organizational psychology or manufacturing are

Different Kinds of Consultants

able to exercise their skills and sell their knowledge in a wide range of operations ranging from small manufacturing plants to the armed services. All consultants must have done something when we had an honest job, so to some degree we can all offer one or more specialisms. It is when offering more than one that the potential difficulty in selling our services arises.

For example, I happen to have had the advantage of working for General Motors at a time when budgets, if not infinite, were at least generous. The result was that, whatever I wished to learn about, I was given the opportunity. At my employer's expense I was able to jet around the world sitting at the feet of gurus, an opportunity for which I am grateful. What is more, having a mind which resembles nothing so much as a sponge, what I learned made me want to learn more, a tendency that I have to this day. The result is that I must to be careful not to present myself as some sort of jack-of-all-trades know-it-all, because clients are wisely prone to believe the old saw about 'master of none'.

There is one problem experienced by narrow specialists, whether they are in human resource or manufacturing management or whatever. Just as there are sometimes informal hierarchies in a business in which, say, marketing or finance is for a time 'flavor of the month' and the recipient of all good things, functional specialisms experience prominence and decline. If you were a human resource expert who had been making a decent living and you found that human resource expertise was no longer saleable, what would you do? Developing a whole new area of expertise is time consuming and expensive and you need to be able to keep putting bread into your family's mouths.

Most consultants faced with this dilemma do one of two things. Either they continue to sell their specialism but invent a new name for it; or, less creatively, they read the latest business bestseller and peddle a fad of the moment as a veneer over their old, unwanted skills. Not all fads are necessarily bad (nor, as it happens, are they very often new), but they are unlikely to be a panacea. When the same snake oil is being pushed to the wrong people by the barely knowledgeable, the results can be disastrous.

Consultancy roles

Consultants are able to play various different roles within your organization.

A consultant, especially a good consultant, is a person of many parts and if you are to manage her effectively you need to know, in the banal phraseology beloved of HR specialists, 'where she is coming from'. One role that most good consultants do not always fill with distinction is that of salesperson. There are exceptions, of course, but by and large, if you are faced by a slick sales barracuda this may not be the consultant of your dreams.

Good consultants are divergent thinkers, anxious to find the best solution in all cases. They find it difficult not to see three sides of a question, particularly where there are only two to the less creative. As a result, many excellent consultants are constrained when it comes to promoting themselves as the answer to a client's prayer – they can see that, good as they are, there might just be a better approach from a more experienced source. I am frequently surprised by the modesty of some of the best consultants I have ever worked with, just as I am often shocked by the arrogance of so many incompetents.

A modern consultant will not be a 'pile 'em high, sell 'em cheap' salesperson of the old school. She may very well be a superior influence technician. If you feel like you are being sold to, the consultant is less likely to be a well-rounded professional. An increasing number of consultants are learning more about the psychology of influence, which demonstrates convincingly that those who want an easy road to the sale are well advised to meet the client's emotional and rational needs at every stage. If you feel comfortable, coming to a purely rational decision unhindered and unpressured by her, she is very probably a very good consultant.

When it comes to playing other essential roles, the modern high-quality consultant is a veritable Sarah Bernhardt. She will give a seamless performance in turn as an expert, an advocate of a preferred solution, a trainer, developer, coach, partner in problem solving, identifier of alternatives, fact finder, supporter and friend.

These roles are important to understand if you really want to manage the intervention. They are even more important for your team to understand and apply sensitively if you decide to cut the cost of change by developing a more or less permanent internal consultancy team.

The roles fall into two major categories, directive and less directive.

Directive roles

Advocate

The advocate is the strongest directive role. Whereas the expert (see below) often proffers advice on a 'take it or leave it' basis, the advocate exercises every subtle influencing skill to ensure that you implement her advice. You may well not fully understand what is happening, but she is gently, oh so gently, pushing you exactly where she wants you to go.

You will only recognize the skilled advocate by looking for very subtle cues. Your feeling will not merely be that you respect her, but that you like her. She will seem either to be just like you or really to understand you at the deepest level. You will want to give her your favorable attention even before she starts talking.

And when she talks she will focus entirely on what you want to achieve, she will make your needs the sole topic of conversation. She may then remind you of what you are up against before she starts to demonstrate conclusively that doing what she proposes will certainly, no room for doubt, give you all that you want and more. Her attitude will be entirely supportive and her logic impeccable and she will have you eating out of the palm of her hand.

If you have chosen your consultant wisely, the greater the ease with which she moves you to implement her ideas the sooner you will reap the benefits. If, however, you want to know how she does it, read my book *The Power of Influence*, where you will learn the proven techniques and understand the research which led to them.

Expert

The expert is also a directive role, but one which is easier to spot. It is not as gross a generalization as it sounds to say that this is a role almost exclusive to men. It has none of the subtlety of the skilled advocate. In essence it boils down to 'I am, in this area at least, your superior in knowledge and I tell you, with all the power of my expertise behind me, that you had better do it my way – or fail'.

I say that men prefer this style because, as Deborah Tannen has convincingly demonstrated, men communicate asymmet-

Different Kinds of Consultants

rically, fencing and feeling for advantage. If I visit you, you may be the President of the United States or the chairman of General Electric, but it matters not, I will try to find a field, any specialism, where I have the edge in knowledge or experience and, having found it, I will exploit it as far as I can.

Expert is a power play – as is status, referent power (someone else's need to be like me and do as I do), the right to apply sanctions and rewards and the relative positions in some hierarchy. Believe it or deny it, most men enjoy power games and consultants have opportunities galore to play many of them.

The best way to test the expert, and of course he may well have all the knowledge he claims and more, is to implement his ideas. Fail to do what he advises and he has the supreme alibi. Do it and fail and he may claim that you simply did it wrong, but that sounds a lot less convincing. So do as he says. Have him advise step by step on the implementation and hold him accountable for the outcome.

Trainer or educator

Trainer or educator is the least directive of the directive roles. Trainers need sensitively to walk a tightrope between being supportive and in control. They cannot afford to relinquish a degree of control or learning becomes, not as Arie de Geus calls it constructive play, but anarchy. At the same time, the best trainers protect and support those who have difficulty learning so that they can absorb knowledge and develop skills in their own time, which is usually the shortest time possible.

This balancing act may be part of the reason that the best trainers I know tend to be women. As a trainer I have no doubt that I would benefit from a little more of the coach and a little less of the controller.

I still shudder when I think of the unfortunate US executive who succeeded in getting me to lose my professional cool. Pressured beyond endurance by his unwavering pride in his total stupidity and ignorance I finally, after several days, told him what I thought of him. I remember that he was slumped so low in his chair that I thought a hole had appeared below him. As I finished, wishing I hadn't spoken so frankly, he looked up, grinned happily, and fed back to me the only part of what I had taught that he seemed to have remembered: 'When faced with unjustified personal abuse, alibi your attacker's behavior so that you can disperse their anger.'

He repeated parrot fashion what I had said, by way of example, only a few moments before: 'I understand your feeling that way, most people do'. But he had achieved something and I had stepped out of line. I would bet that few women trainers whom I respect would have acted so crassly. I would also bet that many of the men who do the job would have done worse – and enjoyed it.

There is more on training in Chapter 13.

Less directive roles

Collaborator

Collaborator in problem solving is a vital role which carries within it rather more team player than expert, but it implies expert nonetheless. I often find that executives, even those trained in problem-solving techniques, fail to understand that there are horses for courses. Rational problem-solving skills which trace the probable cause are most successful when the problem is a deviation from the norm, a situation where what usually happens fails to happen.

Where the problem has existed for a long time, where it seems that something has always been the case and has never been satisfactory, more creative approaches are usually better. Recognizing this, the consultant briefly acts as an expert as she intervenes with: 'This may be a useful approach'; or: 'Have you tried thinking about it this way?'

Once the client group starts down the right path the consultant becomes a team member, or better yet, since the client must own the solution as well as the problem, a facilitator, concentrating entirely on support the process and avoiding the content as much as she can.

Identifier of alternatives

It is the responsibility of any consultant to help the client widen his thinking. She will, through sensitive facilitation, help you to generate as many alternatives as possible so that your chosen course of action is as near to optimal as is feasible.

The role of identifier of alternatives is a key part of the consultant repertoire, one of the many ways in which the good consultant leaves the client more autonomous for the future rather than increasing dependence on external intervention.

The consultant should present any alternatives of her own as a menu from which the client is encouraged and helped to improve on, rather than as a suggestion which 'ought' to be followed. Those consultants who ply their trade in litigious arenas are well advised to develop and perfect this role.

An increasing number of clients are, rightly, suing the purveyors of bad advice; few would believe that they have a case against someone who helped them think more broadly and effectively and provided effective tools for making choices without forcing a fad down the client's throat.

Our work in dominance strategy is the ultimate identifier of alternatives role. Only you are likely to know enough about your business to be certain which customers you must win from the competition in order to strengthen your position while weakening the opposition in the early stages leading towards dominance. Given that you have failed to win them or keep them in the past, we help you identify and apply the key strategy which is unique to your situation and which will work for you.

The directive roles may give the consultant a buzz, but this is as nothing when compared to the joy that comes when a client, sensitively helped and supported, experiences his own *eureka* moment, often after years of honest effort and repeated frustration.

Fact finder

The role of fact finder may be the least directive of all. Encouraging and helping the client to think deeply about his own business and identifying what is crucial from a web of complex data demands that the consultant limits her role, at least initially, to asking follow-up questions which separate the meaningful from the peripheral and providing techniques for organization and analysis. Since research shows that only 6 percent of even the information which relates directly to customers is used in the average organization, and since executives are increasingly concerned about information overload, this is an important function of consultancy.

If Nonaka and Takeuchi are right when they say that the Information Age has already run its course and that we need to perfect a means of turning information into knowledge by combining data with 'tacit' knowledge (the hunches, ideas, feelings and creativity of those closest to the coal face), it will go beyond important and will be a critical source of your competitive edge. The great consultant is one who can, consistently and without undue expenditure of client time, ask the right questions in the right way to bring out the relevant answers just when they are needed.

As well as deciding on the type of consultant you want to approach, you also have to think about whether you want to use a big firm, a small firm or a one-person outfit.

Big firm

Although I have written much about their over-reliance on green beans, there are good reasons for approaching one of the major consultancies. However, don't expect even the least experienced of their consultants to come cheap.

Advantages

- ✔ Worldwide business intelligence into which you can tap when it is appropriate to your situation.
- ✔ Huge resources in terms of people and materials. You never need to worry about your consultant falling under a bus. Continuity is assured as there is always another to take the place of any casualty.
- ✔ With a wide range of specialisms, a single consultancy can offer sufficient people and a broad range of skills to deal with the most complex problems.
- ✔ In-house research capabilities may be of a very high standard.

✔ They have the experience and the expectation of dealing at the highest organizational level and considerable credibility in boardrooms across the world.

Disadvantages

✘ What you see is by no means always what you get. Much of the work is carried out by the less experienced consultants.
✘ Project management is not always of a high order. 'Experience in your industry' may mean that someone has worked for many years in your industry, but more often it means only that he has consulted, on one or more occasions, in your industry. It is your responsibility to find out what exactly is meant.
✘ Sometimes the fees are high and the quality is poor. This does not mean that the individuals concerned are not smart, but they may be woefully short on experience.

Although I would not accuse the best-known consultancies of playing these kind of tricks, I do personally know of situations with certain large firms where the pressure to get as many people as possible out and earning has led to additional consultants being sent, uninvited, to client briefing meetings. They have no other role there than to take up space and time. Injury is added to insult when the client is subsequently invoiced for the 'contribution' that these spectators are deemed to have made.

Small firm

The good, often highly specialized, small firm can offer exceptional service and remarkable value for money. My experience with small consultancies in the US encourages me to believe that in some ways small and devoted bands of specialists led by an exceptional and dedicated entrepreneur-guru can be the perfect model for the industry.

'Can be', however, is far from 'always is' – so although the advantages may be great, there are negative possibilities that must be considered.

Advantages

✔ The small firm needs to cherish its customers. Until it has reached a certain critical mass it needs you more than you need it. There is a tendency, therefore, to provide added value in far greater measure than large firms care to or one-person bands can afford to.

For example, Liese Tamburrino, president of the relatively small but rapidly growing Camden Partners of Barrington, near Chicago, insists that every point for discussion at internal meetings is justified on the basis of 'What does that do for our customers?' If the answer is 'Nothing, it's an internal matter', the item is simply struck from the agenda.

Liese's team produces high-quality market information and massively increased sales productivity, but ask her what business she is in and she replies, 'Delighting and keeping customers'. This kind of commitment is not impossible for the large firm or the one-person outfit, but it is rare.

- ✔ 'What you see is what you get' is a better bet with the small firm than with larger ones. If you want the boss and you are prepared to pay a little more to get her, you are unlikely to be fobbed off with an inexperienced substitute.
- ✔ Costs are kept to a minimum in the small firm. You are unlikely to find yourself financing a Camelot-like corporate headquarters.

Don't necessarily expect a small firm to come cheap, however – the best are highly professional and they know their worth. Nevertheless, if you understand the real difference between 'cheap' and 'economical' there is an excellent chance that the small firm will give you what you need.

Disadvantages

- ✘ Small firms, almost by definition, are going to have fewer human and other resources than their larger brethren. If you expect to have only the principal in your company today and a veritable cast of thousands available tomorrow, at short notice, you will need to call on one of the industry giants. Small consultancies try hard to plug the human resource gap by networking with outsiders to provide a service, but unless they are rigorous and their subcontractors are disciplined there is always the danger that the quality of work falls off.
- ✘ Small firms also have a relative paucity of physical resources when compared to the giants. This is a disadvantage if the job is dependent on having available some sort of state-of-the-art gizmo, but sometimes it is an advantage.

Different Kinds of Consultants

General Electric in the US used to reward success in a somewhat strange way. If an executive and his team exceeded their objectives they were challenged, the next year, to meet tougher goals with fewer resources and a smaller budget. Those who have experienced this hard practical school have learned a massively valuable and enduring lesson. They know how achieve more with less, which would be an ideal trait in a consultant.

✘ If small firms are not busy, their credit line with the bank becomes exhausted. This means that they have little time to have their people trained during the characteristically busy day. The best overcome this by mentoring, sharing up-to-the-minute information and concepts throughout the organization, fostering self-development and encouraging and financing people who are prepared to work evenings to increase their knowledge and achieve relevant qualifications. The best do all this, but they remain a very small minority.

✘ Time is another resource which may be in short supply in the smaller firm. With few people to spare, tight deadlines are the norm and you would be wise to seek evidence that any small firm you hire is capable of being both quick and careful.

✘ Some small firms are a little too specialized. Many consultancy assignments demand an integrated range of skills and knowledge, or as much harm may be done in one place as good is done elsewhere. If you choose a small firm, make sure that they have enough awareness to understand how the elements, functions and specialisms of your business interact.

One person

One of the reasons that I wrote *High Income Consulting* was my deep and abiding concern about one-person consultancy outfits who appear to be offering their services with no professional justification of any kind. Having been a one-man band myself, I must, of course, emphasize that going it alone by no means disqualifies a consultant from serving. Never forget, however, that the lone ranger of consultancy is under constant pressure to put food on the table and keep up the mortgage payments; the temptation to claim skills which are sadly lacking in order to make a crust is never far from the surface.

The potential advantages and disadvantages of the one-person consultancy are generally those of the small firm only more so. If I am all there is, what you see is obviously what you get. I may well come relatively cheaply if I am not a big-name guru with a business bodice-ripper or several to my credit. I may, on the other hand, be pressured by my need for income to accept assignments that I am not qualified to perform.

Many lone consultants pride themselves on being quick learners who can mop up enough in the local library in an hour or two to get by. Others skim the latest business bestseller and within a matter of hours offer themselves as an expert on a fad that is unproven, sometimes from a source that is questionable. This would be less of a problem were it not for the fact that, even if the fad turns out to be pure gold, their knowledge is superficial and their capacity to wreak havoc in your business is immense.

There is, of course, a plentiful supply of highly credible and creditable one-person consultancies. The difficulty is finding them. This problem has not been lessened by government interference in the consultancy market.

Different Kinds of Consultants

Business Links were established by the British government, using the same people, in general, who had already failed to serve business as the Manpower Services Commission, the Training Agencies and Training and Enterprise Councils. The Links were envisioned as one-stop shops for consultancy and training for small business. What they have become, when they have become anything other than a drain down which to pour public money, is a source of really cheap external help and thus the last resort for the virtually unemployable self-styled consultant.

Pushing down the price of professional services of any kind is fraught with problems. Not only does a low-price, high-volume market attract the barely competent, but it also acts like a magnet to the shady and downright fraudulent.

Some years ago the UK Department of Trade and Industry managed an initiative through which small companies could be helped to achieve the quality standard ISO 9000 (in those days BS 5750). I had worked with some major corporations on the quest for quality and my view that formal accreditation was by no means invariably the most economic approach was well known, so my local Chamber of Commerce tended to redirect queries to me.

Many times I picked up the telephone to hear the owner of a small, sometimes very small, business ask if I could tell him about this 'quality legislation'. It invariably turned out that someone had tried to cheat him into spending several thousand pounds on worthless consultancy that he neither needed nor could afford. Their stratagem – the pretence that it was mandatory under some imagined legislation – was greatly facilitated by the fact that these miscreants could imply, since they could access government grants, that they had some vestiges of authority.

Price is never a sound basis on which to make any purchasing decision. I know you can spend all that you have and still get an unacceptable outcome, but if you go for cheap, it is unlikely to be even cheerful. The failure of government-sponsored consultancy is equally the failure of consultant accreditation, since anyone who operates under a government scheme is subject to some kind of accreditation. Once again, buyer beware.

Part II

What's Your Problem?

4

Why Do You Need a Consultant?

We could have come up with the ideas they suggested, but we aren't very creative.

John Madden

IN PART I WE EXPLORED HOW THE CONSULTANCY PROFESSION HAS grown in recent years and the characteristics of the different kinds of consultancies among which a client can make a choice.

But before you can decide on the type of consultant you need, you must have defined the exact problem you face. In this chapter I hope to give some practical advice that will enable you to decide when it is appropriate to bring an external adviser into your business and when it would be better to do the work yourself.

Perhaps I may be forgiven if I start by explaining the principles that I believe should drive your business and mine.

Lambert's law

In *Alice in Wonderland*, Humpty Dumpty says that words mean anything he intends and anything that he repeats three times is true. It seems that if a writer steals something so long ago that he forgets where he stole it from and if he repeats it often enough someone will put his name to it. Thus the following has been called, kindly but erroneously, Lambert's law.

Nothing should be done in a business unless:

- There is a valid business reason for doing it.
- It will repay at least its cost in a reasonable and predictable time.
- It can be fully explained in simple and motivating language to those who will be responsible for making it work.

That is the simple and straightforward philosophy that I believe must underpin the decision of whether or not to hire a consultant.

Do not hire a consultant unless you have a specific and well-understood business reason for doing so and accept that part of the essential understanding is to know the outcomes which you expect and demand.

Many readers will be familiar with Peter Drucker's dictum that the primary goals of a company are to perpetuate itself and to grow, and that to do these things it is essential to find, attract and keep profitable customers.

These are the three valid business reasons that might lead

any company to hire a consultant. Bear with me, if you will, while I examine each in a little more detail.

Perpetuation means survival

The longevity of business has been the subject of many years of research and a recent book by Arie de Geus, *Living Company*. Although there are a few economists who are happy to announce that we have, in some mysterious way, repealed the business cycle, the real world shows that the cycle is spinning ever faster.

De Geus's research indicates that, whereas some corporations last for centuries, the norm is now for companies to last, on average, little more than a dozen years. The average life of an enterprise within living memory used to be 50 to 60 years. In a global economy, any other business, anywhere in the world, is your potential nemesis.

Put simply, this means that in the medium term every business, even those that serve a very limited local area, need to seek ways of becoming and remaining world class in the eyes of those who matter most, actual and potential customers. What is more, they need to become world class at the lowest possible cost. If you lack the knowledge within your business of how to become world class you may, at some time, need the services of a good consultant.

Gary Hamel and Chris Prahalad, in what I am jealously forced to admit is almost certainly the best business book to be published this decade, *Competing for the Future*, have made a compelling case for strategic dominance. If you want your business to survive in a global environment where the ability to get products and services first to market is often the key to success; where there is a pressing need to take and keep control of your organization's destiny because if you don't someone else will; where self-defense demands that you create the shape of your industry in your chosen markets so that your competitors, forced to play a game of catch-up, lose money or withdraw; if you need, in short, a dominance strategy and if you are less than sure that you know how to do these things, you certainly need the services of a good consultant.

And please do not be misled by the use of the word 'strategy' into believing 'We do that'. I see too many 'strategic plans' which are vague wish lists and too many mission statements which are the bland regurgitations of business-school speak to be overconfident about what passes for planning in some corporations.

What I am talking about here is a hard-nosed, practical approach to the market that enables you to take on your competitors head to head, leverage your strengths to strip them of their worthwhile customers and then create and sustain added value such that no one can hope to catch up in the sectors, segments or niches where you choose to operate.

It is not a matter of writing fine sounding but basically meaningless mission statements, of experiencing visions or of completing, and then ignoring, SWOT analyses. It is a matter of taking your markets apart and then putting them back together again so that their needs match your strengths, not just now but for the future. If you doubt your ability to do this, sooner or later you will need the services of a superior consultant. Remember, benchmarking won't do it for you. The need is to leapfrog the competition and stay ahead, not catch up with it.

But there is a real danger in focusing too exclusively on strategic thinking. If your organization cannot survive and prosper in the present then the business may well die before you.

Some of these ideas may seem too grand or too esoteric for you. If they do, you almost certainly need the services of a competent consultant to explain them thoroughly to you and to ensure that you have the competences and capabilities to keep your head above water and then overtake the best in your markets. If you are making money, someone, somewhere is seeing your markets as highly desirable and is planning to leverage their competences to put you at a disadvantage.

What you do not need and should not want is a one-solution grenadier. You may need business process engineering, you may need to become and remain a world-class manufacturer, you may need to empower your people, you may even need to slim down your organization. You may need every one of the new forms of alphabet spaghetti.

At the very least you need flexible, customer-centered tactics to ensure that there is a tomorrow for you to worry about and you need a strategy which will enable you, in the face of the toughest ever competition, to grab the future by the scruff of its neck and bend it to your will. For that we – and I do mean we, consultants and all – will from time to time need the help of external advisers.

One of Arie De Geus's findings about long-lived companies was that they were as effective at learning as they were at innovation and flexibility. Indeed, their ability to innovate and respond flexibly springs from their unusual capacity to learn and to apply that learning. So we all need to become part of a true learning community – and in order to help us do that we may well need a consultant.

Please be sure to note that in every case you need a consultant if and only if you lack the resources to do it yourself. Of course, you may make the strategic decision that you want a consultant even when you have excellent people who could do what is needed, but you have better uses for their time. When you choose to use the services of an outsider it should always be with the specific intention of leaving your team more capable and more autonomous in the future.

Growth

When I work with top teams of major companies helping them to develop dominance strategies, I sometimes irritate them by being a little pedantic. I insist that they define their terms. Experience teaches that it is essential to reduce ambiguity if we are to expect a large number of people to work effectively together towards a shared goal. Peter Drucker is careful to make it clear what he means by growth, and he means a number of things.

He may and does consider growth in the simple sense of getting bigger, but with Drucker simplicity lies in the lucid description rather than in the concept. A company can grow by increasing the number and quality of the people it employs.

After a period of downsizing more and more firms need to grow in this sense, but if the headcount reductions that have been suffered are not to be utterly meaningless, growth must be undertaken without repeating the errors of the past. You need to grow your business through attracting and keeping more and better people. You may need the services of a consultant unless you fully understand how mistakes of overmanning and undermotivation occur.

Economists, not necessarily those who speak of the demise of the business cycle, believe that we are at the threshold of a period of sustained growth in global trade that will far exceed anything we have experienced to date. If they are right, we all need to think about how we will get optimal value from trade growth. If they are wrong, we need to think seriously about how we will take a bigger slice of a possibly smaller cake. Either way, we all need to sharpen our strategic thinking. But there is more.

Trainers have, for at least the last two decades, trumpeted the value of consensus. They have made it sound as if any common denominator, highest or lowest, is the royal road to the best decision making. Research shows that in most circumstances consensus is little more than groupthink – but in a fast-changing business environment, where the past is little, if any, indicator of the future, consensus counts.

The reason is relatively simple: when change occurs rapidly we all absorb information. Some comes from our reading, some from films, television, the Internet or even from training programs. Since no one makes the bridge for us from the snippet of information to the real-world problem with which we may be wrestling, we undervalue or fail to perceive the value of what we know. Only when others contribute their snippets can we begin to put all the pieces of the jigsaw in place.

The result is that in a world in which change is accelerating and knowledge growing, it is difficult, unless you are a consultant, to be a know-it-all. You need the small but vital pieces of information which others have culled unknowingly from so many sources. You may be adept at drawing on the tacit knowledge of what Nonaka and Takeuchi describe as 'the feelings, hunches and ideas' of everybody. If you lack this expertise, you may need to hire a consultant when you aim to improve your people's decision making in rapidly changing situations.

What is more, what we need for the future is knowledge that integrates tacit understanding with data. We need wisdom, combining knowledge with information and acting synergistically on both.

Growth to Drucker also means simply getting better at what you do best. The central process of dominance strategy is leveraging your organization's competences that play the most significant part in delighting worthwhile customers and then applying them to attract profitable accounts away from your key competitors. The loss of these accounts will critically affect their ability to fund the development of their businesses and thus their ability to threaten yours.

One effective way to grow the quality of your business, but only one of many, is through world-class manufacturing. Although this concept started with manufacturing, it can be useful for all parts of the firm and for every type of operation, whether it offers products, services or is not for profit. In outline, world-class manufacturing leads to improvements in:

- cost
- quality
- reliability
- innovation
- flexibility.

Ideally the improvements are generated by the people who do the job on a day-by-day basis. To make it work you will need to set challenging and meaningful targets and then carefully and consistently measure:

Cost
- the percentage increase in inventory turnover
- the percentage increase in productivity per employee/hour/investment dollar
- the percentage decrease in scrap
- the percentage decrease in administration costs
- the percentage increase in return on working capital
- the percentage increase in profitability per employee
- the percentage increase in return on capital employed
- the percentage reduction in process cycle time.

Quality
- ❑ the percentage decrease in the total cost of quality
- ❑ the percentage decrease in defects
- ❑ the percentage decrease in parts returned to suppliers
- ❑ the decrease in the time taken to identify and correct defects
- ❑ the percentage increase in on-time deliveries
- ❑ the increase in your ability to raise prices without loss of sales
- ❑ the percentage growth in the number of actual and potential customers who identify you as a quality operation.

Reliability
- ❑ the quantifiable improvement in equipment effectiveness/use
- ❑ the percentage reduction in customer complaints
- ❑ the percentage reduction in warranty costs
- ❑ the percentage reduction in engineering changes
- ❑ the percentage reduction in service fixes
- ❑ the percentage reduction in product withdrawals and campaigns.

Innovation
- ❑ the percentage reduction in new product speed to market
- ❑ the reduction of R&D costs as a percentage of sales
- ❑ the number of actual and potential customers assessing the organization as a leader in innovation
- ❑ the percentage increase in patents granted
- ❑ the percentage of management time spent in fostering and leading innovation
- ❑ the percentage increase in employee ideas and suggestions
- ❑ new product sales revenue as a percentage of total sales.

Flexibility
- ❏ the percentage reduction in cycle time
- ❏ the increase in the ability of staff at all levels to 'fill in' for colleagues
- ❏ the increase in the number of jobs learned per employee
- ❏ the increase in the sales team's ability to cross-sell
- ❏ the percentage increase in the use of common materials in different products.

If you know how to channel the capabilities, ingenuity and creativity of your people and to set up and interpret a measurement system, or if you don't need this concept, that's fine. If you lack the knowhow and need the system, you will probably need to assign a consultant.

Some US and European manufacturers, when they found themselves threatened by Pacific Rim and, in the early days, cheap electronics manufacturers, chose to concentrate their activities on the upper end of the market. That, too, is growth as Drucker would define it and turning this kind of strategy into into action may, or may not, need the support of a good consultant.

Finding and attracting profitable customers

Increasingly companies are looking for new markets and new customers. Whether you are anxious to enter new markets by, for example, selling through the Internet or whether you want to sell into China for the first time, you may well do it best by hiring a consultant with technical, marketing or local knowledge.

In order to grow in new markets there are certain things

which, at the minimum, you need to know:

Market potential
- The size of the market
- What is driving customer demands
- The maturity of customers, suppliers, products and services
- Level of imports
- Tariffs and tax barriers
- Distribution arrangements
- Levels of demand and consumption
- Gross and disposable incomes.

Competitor analysis
- The key strengths and weaknesses of competitors
- Mergers, acquisitions and joint ventures involving competitors
- Actual or potential new entries into the market
- New products and services
- Problems experienced with current products or services.

Pricing
- Levels of pricing and profit potentials
- Key competitor pricing strategies.

Technology
- Effect of technology on buying and stocking behaviors
- Potential of technology to create new products.

Costs
- Distribution channels and costs
- Labor and employment costs
- Availability of skilled workers
- Availability and costs of raw materials.

Legislation
- Non-tariff barriers to trade
- Licences and patents (and the degree to which intellectual property rights are protected)
- Employment law.

Customers
- Location
- Buying behavior
- Demands and expectations
- Price sensitivity
- Tendency towards risk
- Average size of initial orders – by sector, segment or niche
- Average size and frequency of repeat orders – by sector, segment or niche
- Credit terms expected and taken.

General issues
- Economic and government stability.

The above brief list is neither fully comprehensive nor mandatory. The actual information required will be a function of the market to be entered and the product or service to be sold, but I hope that it is enough to indicate why a growing number of clients seek local advice. Even if you prefer, in markets with

Why Do You Need a Consultant?

which you are fully familiar, to rely on market testing rather than traditional market analysis, there can be little doubt that in new markets competently conducted research saves money, time and misapplied energy.

Some additional reasons for employing consultants or specialists include:

- organizational change
- requiring specialist knowledge, talent or skill
- needing an unbiased, frank opinion on operations, opportunities, strengths, weaknesses or threats related to your business
- company turnaround
- attracting investment
- acquisitions and mergers, or fighting off an unwelcome bid
- cashflow problems
- incorporation or going public
- cover in case of long-term sickness of a key executive
- winning key contracts
- developing key people
- sensitive organizational problems or situations
- changes to law, regulation or codes of practice
- third-party accreditation (e.g. ISO 9000)
- launching new products or services
- looking for competitor intelligence
- seeking contacts within a new industry.

Defining the problem

Defining that you have a requirement for consultancy is not sufficient. You must be able to state precisely and in detail your exact needs and the particular outcomes you are seeking.

The following checklists may help.

Need analysis

- ? What exactly is the need that you must satisfy?
- ? Why is it important to deal with it now?
- ? Can you express the need in simple, unambiguous language so that an outsider can address it economically?

Define outcomes

- ? Assuming an ideal world, what would be your perfect outcome?
- ? Given a less than ideal world, what is the minimum acceptable to you?
- ? Can you quantify the gap?
- ? How much would you be prepared to pay to achieve this minimum?
- ? Would the intervention of a professional take you closer to your ideal outcome?
- ? What leads you to think that?
- ? If a professional tells you that what you wish to achieve is impossible, how will you react?

Why Do You Need a Consultant?

- **?** What is the timeframe within which your outcome must be achieved?
- **?** Do you understand enough of the desired outcome to brief an external adviser clearly?

5

What Are the Alternatives?

You don't hear the bad things about your company unless you ask. It is easy to hear good tidings, but you have to scratch to get the bad news.

Thomas J Watson Jr

WHEN THERE IS A MAJOR BUSINESS PROBLEM TO BE SOLVED, when there is a significant opportunity to be pursued or when widespread change is indicated, you have a number of alternatives:

- ❏ You may hire a consultant and leave the job in her hands.
- ❏ You may hire a consultant and save time and money by having qualified members of your staff do that part of the work of which they are capable.
- ❏ You may forget about hiring outsiders and rely on your own staff, using talented individuals or one or more project teams.

❏ You may set up, train, develop and use your own internal consultancy team on their own or working, initially at least, with an external consultant.

Let us look briefly at each of these alternatives.

Hiring a consultant and leaving it to her

Advantages

- ✔ If you have selected the consultant with care and skill (see Part III), you have the services of a true expert who ought to be able to deliver your desired outcomes in a fraction of the time it would take even the most capable of your own people.
- ✔ You have the enormous potential advantage of having on your premises someone with a global perspective who will, if you are willing, widen and deepen your own thinking.
- ✔ If she is any good, she will make you look outstanding to your peers and, if you have any, your bosses.

Disadvantages

- ✘ Especially when hired in large numbers, consultants can easily spin out of control, doing more harm than good.
- ✘ The good consultants are always expensive and the less good can cost you the future.
- ✘ By allowing them to work alone you will be paying premium rates for the routine work that always exists in any assignment.

Hiring a consultant and having your brightest and best working with her

Advantages

- ✔ This can and should be a massive development opportunity for your fast-track people.
- ✔ Your organization will become increasingly self-reliant and your people will be both more capable and more confident.
- ✔ When confidence and capability increase together you generate huge added value.
- ✔ You win both ways by cutting costs as you enjoy these benefits.

Disadvantages

- ✘ The key people you choose to work alongside the consultant may be better employed elsewhere.

Using only your own staff

Advantages

- ✔ No one from outside ever knows your business as well as your own people do.
- ✔ Insiders are able to predict and avoid political and cultural problems.
- ✔ Since you are paying them anyway, they are relatively inexpensive.

Disadvantages

✘ Insiders may be parochial, going out to bat for their department or division to the expense of the larger operation.
✘ They will seldom have a global view.

Building an internal consultancy team

Advantages

✔ All the essential understanding of your business is combined with an absence of mistaken loyalty to the old department or division.
✔ If they are committed to their new career, the drive for personal and team development will be fantastic.

Disadvantages

✘ They will almost certainly lack process skills.
✘ You may need to bring in a professional external consultant to kickstart the initiative, which will cost you a considerable sum.
✘ It is unlikely that having your own team will totally obviate the need to bring in an outsider when highly specialized knowledge or even a high level of credibility is important.
✘ A prophet may lack honor in his own country – but astute internal marketing will minimize this problem.

The following checklist will help you to decide which alternative is best for you.

What Are the Alternatives?

Consultant or do it yourself?

- ❑ What is the unique special contribution which, at this stage, you believe may best come from outside the firm?
- ❑ Is this contribution likely to ensure a quicker, cheaper and better outcome in both the short term and the long term?
- ❑ If you bring in an outsider, what will you and your team be able to do that will be a better use of your time than addressing the need that you have specified?
- ❑ Will you, or someone you trust, be able to manage the consultant effectively while he is in your business?
- ❑ Given what a competent consultant is likely to cost, is this need sufficiently pressing to be the best use of your financial resources right now?
- ❑ If you are looking to have a consultant solve a problem, have you attempted to resolve it internally?
- ❑ Why did this attempt fail?
- ❑ Would training of your own people in relevant rational or creative problem solving, or any definable area of business skills, give you a better long-term return on investment than hiring a consultant?
- ❑ If you are seeking to exploit an opportunity, have you fully investigated the availability of ideas within your own organization?
- ❑ If you bring in an outsider, will her presence bolster or damage your authority within the organization?
- ❑ If you bring in an outsider, what will be her credibility within the organization?
- ❑ Do you have the in-house skills which would enable you to address this situation?
- ❑ If you bring in an external adviser, are you satisfied that selection of the right person will lead to your own people being able to cope if a similar situation arises in the future – or will using an outsider now probably lead to ongoing dependence?

- ❏ If the job was done internally, would it be a good way to motivate and develop a key member of staff?
- ❏ Is a suitable individual or team available?
- ❏ Do they have the potential and the time?
- ❏ Would addressing this situation be the best use of their time right now?
- ❏ What is the risk inherent in trying to do the job in-house?
- ❏ What is the risk in bringing in an outsider?
- ❏ If your desired outcome is achieved, what would give you the best chance of building on that outcome to continue to strengthen your organization – if you brought in an external consultant or if you did the job internally?
- ❏ Would the initiative have more credibility with your top team if you did it internally or with outside help?
- ❏ What reason have you to believe that the right professional advice is available at the right price externally?
- ❏ Have you any colleagues or contacts who have dealt with similar situations successfully?
- ❏ Could they provide help or advice?
- ❏ Have you considered setting up learning partnerships or strategic alliances with other, non-competing companies to share ideas and solutions?

6

Selecting the Best – Avoiding the Worst

Among the sheep set me a place and separate me from the goats.
Thomas of Celano

EVEN INEXPERIENCED CONSULTANTS ARE OFTEN VERY GOOD salespersons, so clients must be continually on their guard when deciding which consultant is best to solve their problem. The unscrupulous consultant, just like the dishonest salesperson, has become, through nature or experience, adept at misleading even the most wary. This chapter will help you distinguish the best, those who will be a real asset to your business, from the merely smooth talkers.

I remember a director of an international corporation asking me, some years ago, how he could cut through the bull and make a purely rational judgment about which of several competing consultancies to select. His complaint was that each of them, in only slightly different ways, had put on a dog and pony show for his benefit in which they had made concepts leap through hoops with dazzling results. He was riveted by their verbal dexterity, but no further forward in being able to identify why he should award the contract to one rather than any of the others.

It was not a situation where I could glibly suggest that he hire me: I had neither the qualifications nor the resources to do the job. The only answer I could come up with on the spur of the moment was to suggest that he ask which of them was willing to be paid strictly on the basis of the results they achieved. This might frighten off the total no-hoper, but it would do little more than that in the real world. I hope that the suggestions in the rest of this chapter will be of more help.

Try to learn something

The main reason that the consultancy cowboy is able to flourish is that the client often has little or no knowledge of the substance of his problem – if he did he probably wouldn't be hiring a consultant. Believe me, this is not a situation where 'a little knowledge is a dangerous thing'. Research into consensus decision making has shown that, when you are sure of neither the question nor what information is significant, putting together snippets held by a number of people usually leads to a good decision.

First, seek out an expert. Do any of your colleagues, friends, peers in other industries, suppliers, associations or professional bodies have the information you lack, or even part of it? Could you find in magazines or business publications a little infor-

Selecting the Best – Avoiding the Worst

mation which may stand you in good stead if you find yourself needing to outbull the bull merchant? Is there a seminal book on the subject that you can read with a little more intelligence than the inveterate bandwagon hopper? Even a limited amount of information is better than none – it helps you see where something is completely superficial and you may be able to throw the otherwise apparently credible consultant off track by throwing in an occasional fact.

When I was with General Motors, if I had to select a potential consultant or trainer to handle an area of which I was ignorant, I would invite them to a discussion rather than allowing them to make a presentation. In this way I maintained control, in spite of my ignorance, by asking questions. I always arranged to be accompanied by a colleague, preferably one a little better informed than I was. His role was to intervene from time to time with some totally specious but impressive sounding nonsense.

This was a game in which my colleagues took a great deal of pleasure. It is great fun stringing together something that you know to be drivel but that sounds ultra impressive. It is even greater fun when the bull merchant, anxious to fool you into believing that he and your confederate are fellow professionals, agrees with something that is the technical equivalent of 'the slithey toathes did gyre and gimble in the wabe'. This technique is by no means foolproof, but it can catch the unwary and it is worth a try.

Too good to be true

It is a good rule of thumb that if something sounds too good to be true, it probably is. For example, Seward and Gers have proved through research that they can improve the transfer of learning from single figures to better than 90 per cent. If I had not seen the research and they were trying to sell me consultancy services, I would, at the very least, ask the following questions:

- 'What evidence do you have for that?'
- 'Where have your ideas been successfully applied?'
- 'What were the qualified outcomes?'
- 'How were they measured?'
- 'By whom were they measured?'
- 'Have the results been published?'
- 'Do you have a copy I can glance at now?'

I have grown to love this last question. Some years ago I was interviewing a salesperson who was trying to sell me a psychometric test as an aid to recruitment. She had been rather smart in getting my colleague on her side by administering the test to him and making sure that she accentuated the positive findings (an almost certain way to ensure that the results are believed). She was reasonably well informed in the field of reliability and validity and could talk of distributions, z scores and the like without saying anything crass. She was well prepared, but I was not entirely comfortable.

I asked if she had the research paper that demonstrated how the test had been validated. She had. As she handed me the paper one line in the abstract at the top caught my eye: 'For the reasons given this test is inappropriate as an aid to recruitment.' I don't think that this woman was trying to fool us – she probably believed that the test she was attempting to

Selecting the Best – Avoiding the Worst

sell us would greatly improve our recruitment success. Research papers are tedious to read and, to the untrained, difficult to understand. She was probably a fine example of one who is, in all innocence, subjecting the client to inadvertent bull.

Technobabble

Some sales artists use a few too many technical terms to spice up their conversation. If you suspect that the many definitions rolling off the tongue are meant to obscure ignorance rather than enlighten, some or all of the following questions may be useful:

- 'Could you please explain that in simple terms?'
- 'How exactly would that appear in this company?'
- 'What would I see or hear that would tell me that things are working as they should?'
- 'What specific advantages would your product bring a company such as this?'
- 'Who else in this industry has used these ideas?'
- 'With what results?'
- 'Who might I speak to at that company who is as technically naive as I am but who could explain to me the benefits they have experienced?'
- 'How long does it take for benefits to materialize?'
- 'Can you give me an example of immediate payback?'

If the consultant cannot explain her idea in simple terms, you may want to ask yourself how effective she will be at getting her ideas across to those who will need to make them work. In addition, if she claims that the benefits are immediate, remain in skeptic mode. As a rule of thumb most innovations, and probably all innovations that can only be fully explained in technical language, take some time to work.

When you are asking another firm about its experience, it is important not to speak to a 'techie'. They may enjoy anything new and highly technical and be as inclined to bull as the salesperson, or they may have invested a great deal of company money and be loathe to admit to any problems.

Name dropping

Be careful when a consultant gives you an impressive list of other users of her services. As a potential client, I used to ask for a detailed indication of the work that had been done and, if given the detail requested, I would then enquire how I might be sure that my confidential business would not be related to outsiders in a similar manner.

This might seem as if I were playing games, but I quickly learned that many bad consultants would attempt to ingratiate themselves with a potential client by 'sharing confidences'.

If the consultant rightly declined to tell me her client's business I would ask: 'Whom might I speak to there?' I wouldn't speak to the nominated manager, as his interest in making the results of an initiative for which he was responsible sound impressive might make his input of questionable value. Instead, I would find out the name of his manager, or his manager's manager, who might give me something closer to the unvarnished truth.

And be equally wary of consultants who drop the names of well-known people as a means of personal aggrandizement. You can catch the bull merchant by looking her in the eye and saying: 'What a piece of luck. I have been looking for an introduction to Jack Welch. May I use your name?'

Industry expertise

Some consultants will claim a level of experience in your sector that ought to be questioned. This is an area where, for once, the client has a distinct advantage. Few will know the industry better than someone who is already active in it.

I would ask the following questions about a consultant's specific experience:

- For whom did you work?
- When did you leave the company? (If they left a considerable time ago, it would be easy for any manager to test how current their knowledge is. If they left recently you need to satisfy yourself that they are not trying to sell you the solutions that worked in that company, rather than being those most appropriate to your own.)
- What consulting experience have you had in this industry?
- What did you do?
- What was achieved?
- How does our situation differ from what you have found elsewhere in the industry?

More questions to unmask the con artist

I am far from convinced that I was giving bad advice when I suggested that an excellent question for separating the sheep from the goats would be: 'Are you willing to be paid on results?' It may be unreliable, however, for two reasons. First, the more desperate consultants may answer in the affirmative and try to change either the rules of engagement or the method of measurement once she has secured the job.

The other reason has nothing to do with either desperation or bull: the consultants may choose not to work that way for very good reasons. For example, it is not unknown for clients to back out of a performance contract as soon as the consultant has performed to the very highest standards and the cash value of the improvements she has brought about are seen to be higher than anticipated.

There are other general questions that should always be asked. Since some who present themselves as consultants are actually salespeople in thin disguise, it is sometimes worth asking: 'What is your personal experience as a consultant?'

It is not only the largest consultancies that use green beans. Some relatively small firms have recognized the value of the multiplier effect that they are able to bring to principals' earnings. In fact, they is little if anything wrong with using young and bright people as long as they are comprehensively project managed, charged out at an appropriate fee level and used in areas where they have sufficient competence, but this is seldom the case.

The following questions will make it difficult for the silver-haired and silver-tongued bull merchant to give the impression that they are personally yours for the taking when in fact you will only see them when the contract is signed and then when they present their bulky report and final account:

- ☞ 'Who will actually be doing the work at my premises?'
- ☞ 'Do they have recent experience of my industry?'
- ☞ 'How often will I see a principal?'
- ☞ 'Who will that principal be?'
- ☞ 'What is the difference between your charges for experienced and relatively inexperienced people?'

Finally, you may feel that you can avoid bull by insisting on accreditation. Unfortunately this is not altogether true. I ought to be wearing sackcloth and ashes as I write since I have championed accreditation. I have worked for recognition to be based, as it is in other professions, on a common body of professional knowledge which can be tested by examination and practice. It hasn't worked out that way. In the US, Europe and elsewhere some accreditation tells you little more than that the consultant has paid her dues to someone who called themselves an institute or an academy.

Some very doubtful practitioners have some very questionable letters after their names. However, worthwhile organizations are likely to have a strong and active arbitration arm. It may be worth asking the bullish character enthusiastically waving a piece of vellum in your face: 'If things go wrong, does this mean that there is someone who will sort them out for me?'

The avoidance of bull checklist

On the next page is a final checklist to ensure that you do your utmost to separate the sheep from the goats.

- ✔ Have I exhausted, within reason, my opportunities to learn enough to cut through the bull if I have to?
- ✔ Have I made sure that any colleagues with relevant specialist knowledge are actively involved in interviewing the consultant?
- ✔ Have we agreed those colleagues' role?
- ✔ Have I probed effectively for evidence of the consultant's claims?
- ✔ Have I insisted on being told who measured the results being claimed and how they were measured?
- ✔ If the consultant has claimed that her product or service is research based, has she convinced me that the research is meaningful?
- ✔ Has she cut through the jargon and explained things in terms that even a complete novice could understand?
- ✔ Has she convinced me that this fine-sounding stuff has real relevance to my company and my industry in today's circumstances?
- ✔ Has she shown me that she has done worthwhile work for the corporations that she claims to have served?
- ✔ If she claims to know my industry, does she know it as it is now or as it once was?
- ✔ If she would not be ready to enter into a performance contract, are her reasons valid?
- ✔ Have I clarified whether I am talking to a salesperson or a consultant?
- ✔ Has she convinced me that I will get the right level of support from a properly qualified principal?
- ✔ If she claims a qualification, is it relevant and meaningful?

Perhaps the most telling question is this last one, because after all this remains a matter of personal judgment:

- ✔ Do I feel that I can trust and work with this person?

7

Anatomy of a Consulting Disaster

Keep in mind that the consultants often have little to lose. If things work out, they claim credit. If not, they blame employees or changes in management or a host of other problems.
                             James O'Shea and Charles Madigan

IN THEIR EXCELLENT BOOK *DANGEROUS COMPANY*, JAMES O'SHEA and Charles Madigan make some comments about consultancy which, frankly, I hope and believe are mistaken. They describe a world where consultancy is a dark art which whispers or shouts 'do it my way or fail' to a naive business world with the 'primary interest of fattening the treasuries of their consulting partnerships'.

But what is wrong with having faith in your product, giving good service and making a living thereby? Consultancies do provide added value, sometimes many millions of pounds added value – but when their work is substandard the effects can be damaging in the extreme.

That is why both client and consultant have a duty of care. We are all, consultants and clients, seeking to make a living in a highly competitive society, but, contrary to the beliefs of some, we will do it most readily by being open with each other. O'Shea and Madigan are surely right when they say:

> *At its heart, the dark side of consulting is about losing control and the bright side is about keeping a close watch on what consultants are actually doing as opposed to to what consultants say they do.*

But there is more to it than that. It is the responsibility of the client to take the necessary steps to ensure that the organization gets the best possible value for money. Equally, it is the consultant's duty to behave ethically and professionally, which must include watching closely for signs of potential problems from the outset and being prepared to walk away from an assignment if there are strong indications that it will be impossible to perform effectively.

As a preparation for this dual process of close watching, I would like to analyse one of the most dramatic and costly consulting disasters of modern times to see what we may learn. For the facts in the case I shall depend on the research of O'Shea and Madigan; they are journalists and fact is their business. They describe in graphic and dramatic detail some of the most sensational examples of consultancy going very badly wrong. The interpretation and the lessons to be drawn are, however, my own.

Background

> In 1989 Figgie International was a conglomerate with sales of $1.3 billion and profits of $63 million. It had 17,000 employees spread across its 87 companies and divisions. It was doing well, but in the eyes of its founder Harry Figgie, Jr it could and should be doing better. Mr Figgie ought to know – he had been a consultant before building a business empire.
>
> By 1994 Figgie had spent an estimated $75 million on consultancy fees. Sales had fallen to $319 million and losses for the year totalled $166 million. The corporation had downsized to 6000 employees and had sold seven divisions to raise money to pay off its debts. So how could spending $75 million on advice take a relatively healthy company to the brink of bankruptcy?
>
> Figgie's management style was described, albeit by competitors, as 'hire 'em, tire 'em and fire 'em' – and he probably would have taken that as a compliment. He made comments to *Fortune* magazine such as: 'I know how to chew ass' and 'you don't build a company like this with lace on your underwear.'

Avoid 'yes men'

As a client, if your preference is to be eternally surrounded by 'yes men' it is probably asking too much of human nature to expect you to change. But you should be told, at least once, that while you hold that view you will never employ a worthwhile consultant. The client needs to realize that the role of the consultant is to give advice based on an objective assessment of the total situation, or to provide a process which will lead to the realization of potentially more strategic and tactical possibilities. Sometimes you will like the outcome, sometimes not. No one can force you to take advice, but if you don't intend to listen to anything but 'yes sir, how right you are sir', save your money.

Working with the client as a person

The first lesson here for the consultant is that it must be possible to work with the client as a person. You do not necessarily have to like him, but you must, at the very least, share principles and believe that you can respect each other. Figgie's reputation for firing executives not only for failing to achieve bottom-line results but also for holding opinions contrary to his own should have, at the very least, rung warning bells that this was not a client who would naturally incline towards taking advice.

It is the consultant's absolute responsibility to walk away from an assignment, however lucrative, when she cannot work on a personal level with the client or loyally support the client's actions. When, for example, the client who brings the consultant into the organization is the cause of the problem, the consultant must be able to influence the necessary behavioral change. Any doubts about this must be surfaced before the assignment is accepted. If the consultant walks away she should do everything possible to introduce a competent professional who may be able to resolve the personality problem, rather than leave the client at the potential mercy of any consultant who takes my analogy of the prostitute too far.

Cutting costs

> Harry Figgie was an expert at squeezing the costs of his operation. He was publicly recorded as saying that controlling expenses gave the bottom line much more adrenaline than building revenues.

Comfort zones

Any client is likely to have built his success on a few strategies which are within his comfort zone and to which he has become very attached. Introducing a change, however necessary, may cause great resentment within the organization.

One way in which some firms are successful in maintaining commitment during difficult times is to ensure that if there must be an 'enemy', that enemy should be outside the business. The psychology of influence shows that we are more willing to accept the need for change if we believe that change is necessitated by people or things external to our immediate environment and we all tend to accept the dictates of 'authority'. Consultants can be useful in both respects.

Professional influencing skills

Cutting costs is important, but not at the expense of building profitable revenues. The consultant should make it clear to a prospective client that the solution is likely to be complex and to involve a range of activities and ideas. At the same time she should understand enough about human behavior to recognize the value we all place on actions which have succeeded for us in the past and treat the client's views, however shortsighted, with a combination of respect and highly professional influencing skills.

Unless the client can be persuaded to accept that there is more than one way to skin the proverbial cat and that it is the consultant's job to find those alternatives, nothing is gained by hiring a consultant. It is as wrong for a consultant to take an assignment where the client's unwavering, but mistaken, beliefs will hog-tie her as it is to accept a contract which she is unqualified to complete. In either case the consultant is unable to perform and the intervention is a charade.

Fads and 'off-the-shelf' solutions

> During the 1980s corporations were tending to sell off everything but their core activities, partly because of the difficulty of managing non-core businesses and partly because of the gurus' advice that we ought to 'stick to the knitting'. Figgie successfully bucked the trend by continuing to build a widely based conglomerate, but was beginning to lose the confidence of Wall Street.

Greeks bearing gifts

World-class manufacturing, business process reengineering or even downsizing may be required in specific cases, but you cannot know which or what until you really understand what is happening and why.

Only when you are absolutely convinced that the latest fad is the most important thing for your business to be doing right now should you consider hiring a consultant who arrives breathless inviting you to 'feel the width' of the latest outpouring from an ivory tower. Academics and major consultancies spend much of their time trying to develop the great new idea.

You should regard the consultant who offers a product with a fancy name with the same level of mistrust as pre-history looked on the Greeks bearing gifts. The gifts my be exactly what you need, but sign no contracts before you are sure. You may be about to buy an expensive way of damaging your company, offered by a semi-competent but persuasive traveling medicine show.

A unique situation

A consultant looking at this situation ought to consider that it is always possible for one organization to buck the trend either because their operation or their markets are unique or are they simply getting away with being out of step in the short term. Either way, that organization's situation is unique and any consultant peddling 'off-the-shelf' solutions is automatically disbarred from serving.

In the real world of Figgie the first consultant in there was selling 'world-class manufacturing', an excellent concept. But rather than assume that it was right for Figgie, there should have been an analysis of what was being done right and what was changing in the environment which would lead to the need for some changes in that conglomerate's direction or activities. All consultants ought to understand that, although change is often necessary, continuing the status quo is preferred by most clients if it is a viable possibility.

What is more, research shows that leveraging what the business is already doing right is generally much more successful, in bottom-line terms, than introducing new ideas or mitigating weaknesses. Weaknesses which are a barrier to satisfying the needs of profitable customers call for urgent attention, but those apart, the emphasis ought to be on identifying what customers like about doing business with this company, clarifying if other profitable customers are likely to want the same things and then finding ways of giving the market more of what it wants.

The top team

> The opportunity for consultancy on a grand scale at the Figgie corporation arose in part because Harry Figgie, Jr was not perceived as having a succession plan. He chose to appoint his son, Harry Figgie III, to follow him. Harry III had little business experience, in fact he was an orthopedic surgeon by profession, but he was president of Clark Reliance Corp., a family-owned, independent company. Harry III was given the specific responsibility to 'modernize' the company. He was a great believer in modernization, particularly automation, and once told an interviewer: 'We can walk through a plant in ten minutes and tell if we can automate it.'
>
> Whereas Harry Figgie, Jr. was dedicated to the careful control of resources and would not allow any Figgie International executive to spend a cent without rigorous assessment of the effect of new investment on the bottom line, his son was more inclined to spend. He bought equipment without discussing the purchase with the managers who would use it and on one occasion he bought $40 million worth of state-of-the-art machinery at a Chicago exhibition apparently on little more than impulse.

Agree goals

If you are a client in a situation where diametrically different views on important matters are likely to exist within the top team, try to avoid the temptation to bring in a consultant simply to support your view. Try instead to agree specific measurable, worthwhile and time-constrained goals with your colleagues and brief the consultant on these. If necessary, make it clear that the consultant's earnings are performance related.

Discover the reality

The tools of world-class manufacturing, which are mainly those of process improvement and measurement, might have been of real value in Figgie's situation. The consultant would need, however, to be sure that neither Harry III's nor her own enthusiasm was in danger of leading both astray. I would be seriously worried, as any consultant should be, if I felt that in their enthusiasm for automating in one or more places the client was overlooking the potential effect on performance and morale elsewhere.

It is not possible, of course, to know how much information would have been available to the consultants, but the very different attitudes to expenditure should have been easily inferred even from the most superficial and tentative discussions with the client and Figgie's senior management team.

Although it would be tempting for any consultant to side with the spendthrift, especially where their fees are high and likely to grow, it is no part of a consultant's brief to encourage dissension at board level in a client company and it would be incumbent on any professional to attempt to discover how far the elder Figgie's tolerance of his son's profligacy was likely to stretch.

I have always respected, but not yet had the nerve to copy, the behavior of an Australian consultant of my acquaintance. He takes advantage of a quite unjustified stereotype which insists that Australians aren't very bright. In addition to doing his homework about a prospective client, on arrival he asks for directions and then proceeds to turn left where he should turn right. Asking for further directions from anyone that he meets, he also asks the occasional naive questions such as: 'What is it like working here?' or 'What are the bosses like?' The result is that having spoken in addition to a couple of customers and a competitor or two before the meeting, he is able to astound the board with his wide and apparently detailed knowledge of the company.

I am confident that he would have uncovered the important difference in the two Figgies' attitude to money and would have carefully thought through his own role in what might be expected to become a difficult situation. He, and those who have similar good sense, would not find himself in the position of having one principal demanding that he do more and do it faster, while the other was refusing to pay for what had already been done on the rather simple grounds that it seemed to be delivering little if anything by way of result.

The Valdez Team

> Dr Figgie enjoyed action movies. He particularly liked Burt Lancaster's macho performance in 'Valdez Is Coming'. It was a role model of the individual getting things done against the odds, and one which appealed to the doctor's visionary sense. In the presence of consultants he announced that he had established his own Valdez Team, indeed those in the room had been co-opted. This was to be a 'take no prisoners' grouping of managers, executives and vendors who would modernize the company against all odds. He made it clear that anyone who attempted to oppose this team was to be 'mown down' just like the bad guys.

'How' without 'why'

The client is right in seeking to build a cohesive team through a strong vision and a common language, but if the vision and the language are such that the role of the consultant is limited to nothing more than the 'how' without consideration of the 'why', you will certainly get less than optimal added value. Worse, if the consultant feels strongly that the way things are being done is detrimental to the business, you will be reliant on her telling you in a way which does not cause you to lose face, and that may be difficult.

I well remember the difficulty of attempting to reinstate a corporate executive who was unwise enough to threaten more than he could deliver at a major company conference. When he announced that those who did not unthinkingly support his grand vision would be given the DCM (don't come Monday), the audience of managers laughed and he was gratified by the effect of his witticism.

Unfortunately, they were still laughing after the meeting at the foolishness of an executive who was widely known to avoid risk at all cost, who played the Rambo role badly and threatened sanctions he was powerless to impose. If you threaten, you had better be able to deliver and it had better be in the interests of the firm that you do so.

Someone who handled this kind of thing effectively was Robert Townsend, one-time savior of Avis. He believed that, in order to demonstrate that things really were going to be different, as a new CEO charged with the job of saving the company he should remove a significant and well-known human barrier to progress as quickly as possible. He fired someone who was known to everyone to be a pain in the butt and he did it, not for his own aggrandizement, but in order to get essential things done before it was too late. If a consultant uncritically supports trivial acts of machismo on behalf of her principal, it is usually safe to assume that her only real interest is neither the client nor his company. It is her fee alone which is dictating her actions.

Minimizing casualties

The consultant's position here is invidious. On the one hand it is right to commit yourself to the client team with which you are working even though you can only be a temporary member, but you need to keep a cool head and I would hope that the professional would consider to what degree she could maintain objectivity in what appears to be a test of machismo. It is the consultant's duty to help the client achieve his dream, but it is an overriding duty to minimize casualties at the very least.

Failure to hit targets

> Although Harry III wanted change, which means taking risks, the outcome of failure to hit targets remained as it always had been at Figgie. Executives made the profits demanded of them at the time specified – or they were fired.

Delivering benefits quickly

The consultant would not need to be much of an expert on change management to understand that the early effect of change, even beneficial change, tends to be a temporary fall-off in performance. If the reaction to that fall-off is to introduce a further major change, such as firing the manager, the chances are performance will plummet. It is the consultant's duty to ensure that changes can be assimilated and start to deliver benefits as quickly as possible. That means changes should be introduced either a little at a time or all together in a single package, and sufficient time should be given for them to take effect. Too often the consultant is the first to panic when changes fail to deliver immediately.

There is more, but...

There is a mass of detail in O'Shea and Madigan's book from which I could draw more lessons for consultant and client. In due course the car parks at Figgie International overflowed with the cars of consultants and accountants. Accountants were checking the work of consultants, consultants were continuing to be perceived as wasting management's time. Work teams were organized and reorganized in some cases as many as eight times in a few weeks. Consultants demanded time-consuming meetings at which, according to the Figgie executives, the burden of their discussion was 'What should *we* do next?'

If you want to know the whole sorry story, I recommend you read the book. One more thing, however.

Perhaps the most telling aspect of the tale is encapsulated in this short quotation:

Anatomy of a Consulting Disaster

> *Lawson and Giffi [two lead consultants] who hadn't been made a partner yet, also looked around at Figgie International and noticed many other problems that could use some consulting.*

This was kind of them, of course, and doubtless the information was valuable. If I may suggest one more thing to clients: when this happens to you it might be a good idea to remind the consultant that you are not paying her to shake the bushes for more business and, much as the information is appreciated, full attention to the job in hand might serve your present purposes better.

Part III

Managing the Consulting Process

8

Finding the Right Person

If you think that your client is stupid, remember you wouldn't have the job if he was any smarter.

Albert A. Grant

IF YOU HAVE DECIDED TO EXPLORE THE POSSIBILITY OF HIRING a consultant, you need to find the individual or the firm which is right for this job in your company as it is right now.

Your company culture and even your staff's success record may have a great deal to do with your choice. For example, your people may have a poor record in dealing with similar situations to the one you face. This increases the likelihood that you will need a consultant, but it also means that you need a special type of person, or a person with a special type of knowledge.

To get the result that you want with the minimum amount of hassle in the minimum time in these circumstances, you need to find someone who understands the dynamics of losing teams.

You may have a culture in which people have been empowered. Successful empowerment often leads to teams which make their own rules, cover for each other in times of illness or absence and, in the interest of cohesiveness, oppose the introduction of newcomers even when there is a clear need for help. They may react to the outside adviser by closing ranks. Your consultant needs to understand this and respond sensitively to the very natural way that people behave. If they don't understand the situation they are unlikely to succeed.

Identifying possible candidates

Where might you start looking for a suitable consultant?

Previous consultants

If you have used consultants successfully before, it is good practice to ask them first (for the benefits of this, see the discussion in Chapter 9). Be open with them: if you do not feel that they are up to the job, say so, but ask if they know of others who have the requisite skills.

The consultant may, of course, try to persuade you to use their services again. They may have skills and offer services which would surprise you. Clients often assume that a consultant is limited to whatever she has successfully done for the organization in the past, but the fact that she was superb in market research does not necessarily mean that she does not show equal expertise in training, strategy formulation or facilitation.

Even if she agrees that she is unqualified to do the present job, she may be able to introduce you to someone who is highly qualified. This is lucky for you, in that it saves you time and you can arrange things so that your previous consultant can act in a project manager role, making sure that the consultant she introduced performs to the high standards required.

She should be paid to do this, of course, but not directly by you. The consultant she recommends has greatly reduced the cost of marketing and selling her services through this introduction. What is more, if you choose to hire her she has sold time which might otherwise have brought in little or no income. She should therefore be prepared to pass on, say, 20–25 percent of her fee to the person who pointed her to this additional business.

Referrals

Seek referrals from others you know and trust. Most of us in business have a wide-ranging network of contacts and we aware of their competence and reliability. It is easy to call on the most reliable and ask if they have used consultants, what exactly the consultants achieved and whether they would recommend them for further opportunities and, if so, what kind.

You do not even have to say what you want the consultant for if the assignment is highly confidential, because even if recommended consultants lack the immediate skills you require, they too will either belong to a large firm with many arrows in its quiver or have a network, or both. They can be an excellent source of information even when they cannot serve and they too have a vested interest in your satisfaction: if you use consultants once you are likely to use them again.

Other sources of information

It is always worth reading the business press and the trade and financial journals when you have a problem on your mind. It is amazing how often it seems to be on other people's minds as well. You may find authors who appear to know what they are talking about and are often consultants you can talk to or, and this is better yet, you might just find the information you need to tip the scales all the way back in favor of doing it yourself. Either way you have won.

You may be a member of a professional association or trade group. Attend their meetings to listen to the better speakers. Pick their brains. Ask around in general terms and you may be astonished at the number of pointers you receive towards competent consultants. Intelligent speakers will ensure that you know how to contact them even if the crush of admirers stopped you from doing so at the meeting.

The best will not hand out business cards alone or accompanied by a brochure, they will give everyone at the meeting something of value. It may be economic or business data, it may be a copy of an information-rich newsletter, it may be a simple psychometric test. It will be something designed for you to use and use again, and it will have contact details for the speaker. From this you will easily get an idea of whether and how the consultant has handled situations which have some relationship to yours.

There may be a government-backed organization staffed by effective businesspeople committed to providing a service to organizations such as yours and qualified through ongoing learning to do so with efficiency and at little or no cost to you.

It will not take long to find out for yourself, so give whatever you have locally a try. But please remember that consultancy or training on the cheap is worth no more than you pay for it.

Talk to local colleges and universities and take a look round their libraries. They will, of course, try to sell you their services, sometimes very cheaply and sometimes at a wildly inflated fee, and that may be the solution you need. However, even if an academic solution is not for you, the information they unwittingly provide may be helpful in your search or may enable you to reconsider a 'do it yourself' strategy.

Good registers of consultants are few and far between, but if you can find out about one use it. Also something of a rarity is the consultant's broker or agent, but where they do exist they offer the clear advantage that they have every reason to want to link you with the best person to meet your needs. They only get paid by a consultant on their books who wins the assignment. The usual fee paid by the consultant to the agent is around 25 percent of her earnings. If she uses an agent with any frequency her daily rate will reflect this. If, however, an agent places her with regularity, she may well be worth every penny she charges.

One last thought. Just for a while ask your personal assistant or secretary to refrain from throwing out unsolicited mail. The very person you need may be sending you a note at the very time you are beginning the search for her. Stranger things have been known to happen in business.

Evaluating the possibles

Once you have found one or more prospects to talk to, you need a game plan for evaluating each consultant's potential. I suggest that you investigate the following areas, but before you take them from the page, consider your specific needs and identify those which are essential. By way of example, I have taken the more usual requirements and arbitrarily chosen a few as essential.

The key thing about these essentials is that any prospect who fails to satisfy you on any one of them is automatically disbarred from the assignment, so don't make everything an essential unless you are prepared for a long search.

Those characteristics which are important but not essential I have given a weighting from 1 – very low importance – to 10 – almost essential. The idea is that you should be able to:

- exclude immediately those who cannot hope to meet your requirements
- make a quantitative comparison of capability between those who satisfy the essentials on the basis of their ability to meet your most important needs.

Essential

- ✔ The consultant has successfully completed an assignment of this type before.
- ✔ She is qualified for the assignment.
- ✔ She is not wedded to particular solutions or products and her advice is likely to be impartial.
- ✔ She agrees to be bound by your desired outcome.
- ✔ She understands how business works and demonstrates a practical knowledge of human behavior at work.

Desirable

10	The consultant does not confuse 'similar' situations with 'the same'.
10	She has a working knowledge of our industry.
10	She has convinced me that the future autonomy of my business will not be threatened by the style of her intervention.
8	She has already suggested a series of regular meetings at which I will be updated on progress.
8	She will provide me with regular information enabling me to brief the board accurately on progress.
8	She has time to give the job her full attention.
6	She has convincingly explained areas where she can offer added value.
6	She avoids discussing other clients' business and protects confidentiality even when I try to tempt her to be indiscreet.
5	She appears to be personally committed to this task.
5	She appears to be personally committed to me as her client.
5	She listens.
4	She appears to have strong analytical and problem-solving skills.
4	She looks and behaves like a professional.
2	I feel I will get on with her and be able to work with her.
2	There will be necessary backup if she steps under a truck during the assignment.

Having established your needs and prioritized them, while interviewing potential consultants you can score each on the basis of their answers to your questions as you probe for evidence of each characteristic. By multiplying the score that you award to each prospect by the weighting you have given each area, and totaling and comparing each individual's set of scores, you will have a numeric indicator of who best meets the requirements that you have identified and prioritized.

If you have a gut feeling at the end of the exercise that you would prefer to choose someone who is not the top scorer you may choose to go with your hunch. But if you do, you owe it to yourself and your organization to review your initial requirements and the importance you gave to each.

If you cannot see a reason to change your priorities then your hunch is wrong and in following it you will probably make the wrong choice. If your priorities as indicated in the weightings are no longer valid, you made the wrong choices at the start and need to be sure that you do it better next time.

Remember, don't copy either my choices for the essential requirements or the weightings that I have given the remainder – indeed, don't even copy the requirements without a good deal of thought. Consider your unique situation and list your specific requirements, prioritizing them carefully, and you will make a good decision in difficult circumstances.

Finding the Right Person

Questions which should always be asked

Many of the questions that you ask a potential consultant will reflect your specific and unique needs, as discussed above. However, the questions below should *always* be asked to extract the information you need.

You also need to bear in mind the guidelines given in Chapter 6 on avoiding consultants who are merely clever salespeople.

- ✔ What do you see as our principal need or problem?
- ✔ What is it that leads you to that conclusion?
- ✔ What in particular is the evidence which leads you to that conclusion?
- ✔ What specifically do you believe that you can offer that others cannot?
- ✔ How would you wish us to measure your success?
- ✔ Would you be willing to work on a performance basis, earning a share of your success?
- ✔ If so, how would you see such a contract working?
- ✔ If not, why not?
- ✔ What experience do you have in working with an organization like ours?
- ✔ How did it compare in terms of:
  - industry?
  - size?
  - style of leadership?
  - maturity in the industry?
- ✔ What experience do you have of our industry?
- ✔ What success have you had working with problems similar to ours?
- ✔ In what ways do you suspect at this stage that our situation may be different from what you have just described?

The proposal

You can tell a great deal about the quality of a consultant by the proposal you receive. A professional proposal will tell you:

- What is to be done
- Why it must be done.
- When it will be done.
- How much it will cost.

The best consultants have a simple approach to giving you this information. Because it is essential to every assignment, they will have developed a way of providing it with maximum clarity using the smallest possible number of words.

What is to be done

I prefer to present this as a simple flowchart of key activities (examples of a flowchart and a Gantt chart are given in the sample proposal on pages 169–72). Nothing which appears on this chart is anything other than essential. I draw it by starting at the destination, the outcome that my client desires, and work backwards to where we are today. In this way I can be sure I leave out nothing which is crucial to success, but at the same time I put in nothing which is superficial or unnecessary. I show graphically where two or more activities can be done simultaneously and so have a reliable route map for timing the project. But there is more to it than that – importantly, I only show *what* is to be done not *how* it will be done.

One way to recognize the less than professional consultant is that they provide not so much a proposal as a recipe. What we sell is the 'how to'. It is our stock in trade and if we choose to give it away in an effort to look super smart we deserve what we get.

What we sometimes get is a client who may, for clients are not always paragons, either use the unnecessary recipe to have the job done by one or more of his own people, or more depressing still pass it to a friend from the golf club who does a little cut-price consultancy to finance his spending at the nineteenth hole. So look at the proposal: if it tells you more than you need to know you have an opportunity for free or cheap consultancy. You also have a consultant who probably needs the work a good deal more than she deserves it.

The last reason I use the flowchart is to handle the situation in which the client tells me that there is simply not enough money in his budget to pay for my services. Try this with your prospective consultants and consider what they say.

Some ask what you have to spend, swallow hard and offer to do the job for a cut price which just happens to coincide with what you have just said. The quickest answer to this is to say goodbye. If a consultant is willing to do the job for far less than her original quotation, there are only two possibilities. Either she are desperate for work, in which case if you are sadistic you may choose to have fun seeing how far you can push her. Or she was 'flying a kite' with her first bid, which means you can't trust anything she says subsequently.

Faced with your inability to pay what I have asked, I spread my flowchart in front of you. Having made it clear that my daily rate is not negotiable, I suggest that we work through the essentials together to see where money could be saved if you were to take on some of the work yourself. There are often activities which either a member of your team can do the work or someone less expensive can assist me, reducing the cost of my intervention.

This will often give you much better value than you realize. One of your people, having learned from me this time, may be able to do the job themselves should a similar need arise in the future. Your limited budget may well push you into a situation where the development of your brightest people is accelerated and their motivation and job satisfaction is substantially increased.

You will understand, I hope, that if we agree to your people taking on essential tasks I will write precisely what they are to do and when they must have it done into our contract. I have no wish to be kept waiting for key inputs if you decide that it would be an easy solution to another problem to use my designated assistant elsewhere for a while. In my profession time really is money. My time and the skills and knowledge which I apply on your behalf while using that time are all that keep me and poverty at a respectable distance from each other. What is more, if I am any good, my future time is being prebooked and I cannot afford to risk my availability at a key moment because one of your staff failed to get work out when promised.

You stand to gain enormously from using my services or you should not have hired me. Return on any investment should be realized as soon as possible. We have a mutual desire to get the job done as quickly as the quality outcome we both need allows.

Why it is to be done

Behind the flowchart of activities, the knowledgeable consultant will write, for each action, a list of benefits. In short, she will make it easy for you to see what is in it for your organization and why every activity is essential. Your knowledge of the relative importance of each and the way that doing one effec-

Finding the Right Person

tively plays a part in creating the growing benefits which accrue through each successive activity will help you, if funds are limited, to judge those that you are willing to entrust to anyone other than the consultant you have chosen.

A good consultant will do more than that, of course. She will enable you to complete an informal or formal cost–benefit analysis. From this you will be able to tell if the game is worth the cost of the candle.

When it will be done

Most clients have a strong view of when they want a job to be completed. The good consultant will therefore produce a Gantt chart to show that she will meet the agreed goals in the specified time and she will expect your agreement of the timeframe to be equally binding on both of you.

There are, of course, exceptions. Some consultants, or more usually green beans, come to your premises not with the intention of meeting your predetermined objectives in the minimum time consistent with the highest-quality outcome, but with a very different priority. Their first and most pressing aim is to identify the next assignment – your present needs and the work for which you are paying is secondary. If your consultant is vague about timeframes once they have been properly briefed you should be suspicious. If, once hired, they appear to be focused on problems irrelevant to the task in hand, you should bring them swiftly to heel.

How much it will cost

A professional proposal will hold back the cost until you are assured of the value you will receive. This is why I would always prefer to present a proposal in person rather than entrust it to the post. That way I can be sure that you don't peek at the price before you understand the value. I do, of course, breach my own rules on occasion.

I was once invited to forward a proposal to the US when I was focusing my activities in Europe. Loath to pay an air fare when the situation was speculative, I mailed my detailed proposal. I was quickly invited to meet the board of directors. This was important potential business to me and I worked very long hours developing my proposal into a comprehensive and, I believed, compelling verbal presentation. I created beautiful visuals, far more impressive than I could afford at that time. I spent days rehearsing my presentation so that I was both word and nuance perfect.

The CEO greeted me warmly, as did his fellow directors. The omens could not have been more propitious. I felt wonderful and the way the CEO introduced me made me feel better yet.

> *Well, ladies and gentlemen, you have all had time to consider Tom's written proposal and I know that you agree with me that he has hit the nail squarely on the head with a clear and concise outline of precisely what we ought to be doing. Have you anything to add, Tom?*

I should, of course, have added nothing other than a polite request that they sign the contract and name the start date. Instead, overwhelmed by what I saw as my own cleverness, I gave them my whole spiel. I spared them nothing. I showed them every visual and explained every key point in intricate detail. Needless to say, I talked my way out of the contract and showed how adept I could be at snatching defeat out of the jaws of victory. I lost an important business opportunity and I deserved to lose it.

If a consultant prefers to deliver her proposal by hand and talk you through it, sight unseen, give her a point for professional behavior. But if she fails to listen when you tell her she has the job, she deserves what she gets – in my case nothing.

When a consultant says 'no'

You may have a perception of consultants in which we are among nature's most rapacious creatures who never turn down the opportunity to make a buck. I hope by now you understand that it is a mark of the true professional to turn down business rather than take on anything which may undermine their reputation.

If a client is known as someone who tries not to pay his bills or who delays payment up to the courtroom door, no consultant worthy of her hire will be seen to be working for him. Similarly, if she doesn't like your face, your attitude or the job and is sure that she cannot build a professional working relationship with you, she will turn down the assignment. In these circumstances she will grasp at anything which will get her out of the door with the minimum of embarrassment all round.

There are, however, occasional situations where you may wish to try to interpret the consultant's reason for turning the job down. The inept may simply try it on, pretending to be less than keen or too busy in the hope of wringing something out of you. Forget them. If you are not absolutely devastated by her refusal, just get up from your seat and politely show her to the door. It can be amusing watching her trying to wriggle her way back in, but harden your heart. This business is too important to let anyone play games.

Further reasons which consultants give for turning down an assignment include the following:

I don't do that. This is a bad choice if it isn't true. Imagine the consultant's chagrin if she hears that the client has been asked by a business acquaintance whether he knows Ms X, the consultant, and after being told why they are asking he says, in all innocence, 'She doesn't do that, she told me only the other day'.

I'm too busy. It is possible that this is true, but it might also mean 'offer me more money and I'm yours'. The good consultant regards her daily rate as inviolable and she doesn't need to use this excuse, so there is no point discussing it further. (Unless you are like the client who offered to double my fee if I could find and pay the extra to someone equally well qualified to take some of the load off my shoulders. I did.)

I'm afraid it would be a conflict of interest. If this is said, stop the discussion, don't try to find out why, don't give any further information, just thank the consultant for her honesty and say goodbye. You might be wise to ask if she knows someone you might speak to, because the chances are that you are talking to a true professional and, although she can't help with this assignment, her advice concerning those who could may well be invaluable.

Finding and assigning a consultant is a matter worthy of deep thought. It is never easy, but it can be the quickest route to building a fortune or to survival in a difficult business environment. It should be done seriously and with the expectation of success. Having found the right person, her fee is immaterial in comparison to the benefits which she will bring. Find the right person and believe me, the price is right. However, there is discussion of what the fee and the contract should contain in Chapter 10.

Now that you have chosen the right consultant for you, the rest of Part III will consider further aspects of the consulting process.

9

Referees, Referrals and Repeat Business

If I give you a name will you promise to let me know if he fails to say something nice about me? I'll delete him from my Christmas list.

Howard Shenson

MANY CLIENTS CLING TO AN AMAZING DEGREE TO THE IDEA THAT a reference makes them safe in their choice of consultant. Nobody in her right mind would dream of giving as a reference the name of someone who is not guaranteed to speak well of them. I have to add that if you feel that you need to ask me for a reference, I am simply not the consultant for you.

The very fact that you need to push the responsibility for your choice on to someone else means that I have not done the first and most simple part of my job correctly. I have failed to convince you that my personal status and professional credibility are things on which you can rely – totally. If I cannot do this, how can I expect us to build the immediate sense of mutual trust which is essential to developing the most appropriate and economic solution to your problem? I have also failed to persuade you that my intervention *will*, not may, solve your problem or enable you to exploit an opportunity to the greatest effect in the shortest possible time. If my influencing skills are in such poor health when it comes to what I know best, myself, how can I expect to be able to influence your behavior in an area where I have much less knowledge, your business?

There is another reason I will not provide you with a reference. I was trained to believe that everything I do for a client is confidential, and that includes, unless he specifically requires it to be otherwise, the fact that he has ever hired me. Total confidentiality demands that nothing is discussed or alluded to which might give even the smallest part of the game away.

Nevertheless, let me offer a few ideas to those clients who will ask for references come hell or high water. Always assume that the first name given has been the consultant's best friend from childhood, was best man at her wedding and that at some time in the past the consultant saved his sanity, his marriage and his life. Assume, in short, that unless you have have interrogation skills envied by the KGB and all the time in the world to apply them, such a reference is unlikely to tell you what you want to know. What it will tell you is what your putative consultant wants you to know and that may not be nearly the same thing. I can't be the only consultant in the world who, in my very early days when I thought that references were essential, asked my few but enthusiastic clients to do me this favor only to get the response: 'You write what you want and I'll sign it' or 'Just fax me a note of what you want me to say and I'll call him.'

If you persevere you may find, way down the list of references, that honest artist who will paint the consultant's portrait warts and all, but if you were willing to assume such a time-consuming task your doubts about the consultant are presumably strong and you are probably about to make an expensive mistake.

If you work for a government there will be detailed rules about how many references must be demanded and possibly even checked. This might prove a useful model were it not for the fact that in so many countries, for example the UK, the US and South Africa as well as eastern Europe, government expenditure on consultancy has been largely wasted and there are allegations of widespread and serious fraud even in such simple areas as training to enable the unemployed to reenter the world of work. So much for the references.

But if you cannot or will not make a decision without references:

- ❏ Put little reliance in written references.
- ❏ Telephone to discuss the consultant's work with the referee and write down your key questions in advance.
- ❏ Think carefully about follow-up questions:
    - 'How much exactly did you save/make?'
    - 'How did you make it?'
    - 'What precisely was the consultant's contribution?'
    - 'How was it measured?'
    - 'Was the measurement audited and confirmed by a third party?'

Give me a referral – please

After the assignment, rather than asking you to provide a reference a consultant may ask for a referral to another organization.

When a consultant has served you well, has delivered the pre-determined outcomes and done it in the agreed time or more quickly, then, frankly, you owe her. Unless you were both naive she will have delivered ongoing value far greater than the fees which you have paid her. She will have left your organization not only in good shape, but also more autonomous for the future. You or other important members of your team will have learned much which you can apply and reapply again and again in the future to your company's and your own benefit. In short, you have had a great deal.

If you want your consultant still to be around so that you can enjoy more added value in the future, now is the time, purely as a matter of self-interest, to pay your dues. Think hard about who else you know who could benefit from the type of service you have received. Who, in your own organization or outside it, has similar needs, problems or opportunities?

Referral professionals work to a system:

- They ensure that you are delighted with the outcome.
- They go further and delve to be certain that there is nothing they could have done which might have added to your delight.
- When and only when you express yourself to be gratified to the ultimate extent by their endeavors will they ask for referrals.

But they will not stop with the asking, they will:

Referees, Referrals and Repeat Business

- Offer to minimize any trouble which you might take in promoting their work by writing and rewriting any letter or memorandum to be sent to the prospect until you are wholly comfortable signing it.
- Write anything which is to go to a third party in such a way that it emphasizes your achievement and makes it clear that they were little more than the means by which you achieved your considerable accomplishments. (They want you to think deeply and send out as many referral letters as possible.)
- If they take the matter of referrals as seriously as they should, they will even take responsibility for buying the stamps and mailing what you have 'written' on their behalf.
- If you suggest that they should simply contact someone direct – and relatively cold – using your name by way of introduction, they will ask why you think the prospect might benefit from their services. Then they will provide you with something useful to that person, an article, a handout or some relevant data with an appropriate letter to accompany it, so that you and not they appear to knock on the door first.

They will always prefer a referral to a reference and will do all they can to make it easy for you. They know that if they contact a potential client singing their own praises, their credibility is dependent on earlier marketing and luck. But when they are presented as the 'friend of a friend' supported by real achievement, an invitation to serve is far more likely.

Why don't some clients give referrals?

Others, at least equally good at doing the consultancy work, will not take such a systematic view of getting referral business. They will hope, but they will not ask. One of the reasons is that they are sensitive to your needs and they will not want to push you into the embarrassing situation of saying 'no'.

Research shows that the majority of clients do not give referrals regardless of how delighted they are with the service they have received. That is a pity, not just for the reasons I have already stated, but also because referral work needs far less selling and marketing, in some cases more than 80 percent less, and the less selling and marketing the consultant has to do the less they need to charge for their services, giving even higher client value.

So why are most businesspeople, almost certainly yourself included, unwilling to provide referrals?

- ❑ Clients are concerned that they lack the ability to judge in absolute terms the value of what they have received. They may think it was excellent, but they do not know if it was optimal. They fear that giving a referral may deprive their friend, acquaintance or colleague of the opportunity to find an even better solution in the open market.
- ❑ Although they may believe that their situation and that of the other business is similar, they recognize that they are unlikely to be the same. What if the consultant treats them as if they were the same and applies the wrong solution?
- ❑ Finding addresses, telephone numbers, writing letters and making the call is something of an effort. What is more it seems an unnecessary effort, so people don't make the call or write the letter.

- ❏ They are not asked for a referral. Surely it is reasonable to conclude that what your consultant doesn't ask for, she doesn't need.
- ❏ They simply don't want the good results that they have experienced to be available to others.
- ❏ Sometimes referrals are not forthcoming because the client genuinely tried, but couldn't think of anyone who, at the time, would benefit from such a service.
- ❏ The consultant failed to maintain contact.
- ❏ Occasionally the client finds that, in spite of their success in working together, he doesn't really like the consultant and doesn't want to help her.

Everyone of the above sounds, and is, perfectly reasonable. Good could always be better, situations are sometimes more different than they appear to be at first blush, giving referrals is extra work and so on.

But please think of the alternative. The consultant only earns when they are working on a client's behalf. If you are delighted, then it is in your interests to become an advocate of the excellence you have received. If we fail to help those who have truly earned and deserve our support, the mediocre rather than the meek will inherit the earth. And just try shifting the mediocre once they have wormed their way into your business.

Repeat business

Some consultants fight my claim that an external adviser should always leave the client more self-reliant and more autonomous than he was when they were assigned. Some even put into place systems or processes which the client cannot hope to be able to make work in order to have a job for life. Such behavior is quite unacceptable, but, given how some clients behave, it is understandable.

In general, I only visit clients if they have initiated the invitation as opposed to soliciting the opportunity to serve. When we are talking I always ask whether the client has used consultants before. Clients who have used consultants before are more likely to use them again, even if they were dissatisfied with the previous performance. When they tell me that they have used consultants, I ask how satisfied they were. This is the odd part. They often tell me that they were absolutely delighted. So why, I ask, are you talking to me and not them?

I hope that you are as surprised and horrified as I am to discover that they are not talking to me because the task is beyond the competence of their previous, highly satisfactory consultants. Nor are they moving into a different field of activity where my insights will be of unique value. They have not even been seduced by my books, reputation or high daily rate. They have come to me because they fancied a change.

It is not difficult to understand this search for novelty if it is driven by the client's inability to differentiate between satisfactory and optimal results. On the face of it to try someone different may seem to make sense, but this is misleading. From a position of sublime ignorance, how can the potential client be confident that I will not perform worse than my predecessor? After all, part of the cost of using my predecessor was in educating her about the business. Is there any sense in starting the learning curve at the bottom again unless you have an absolute certainty that the results of the intervention will be significantly better?

Of course, there are times when a change is not merely desirable, it is demanded, but the need of the task should have precedence over the *ennui* of the executive. Circumstances in which a different consultant may be required include the following:

- ❑ If the job to be done is beyond the capability of the previous consultant.
- ❑ If the new consultant brings special capabilities or knowledge which is essential to the desired outcome and which cannot be acquired elsewhere.
- ❑ If, in retrospect, it is discovered that the performance of the previous consultant was marred by ignorance in some important field.
- ❑ If the current job requires contact at an organizational level at which the previous consultant would not, for whatever reason, be acceptable.
- ❑ If, at the simplest level, the previous consultant is unavailable to complete the work within the timeframe.

If any of these is the case, a change may be indicated. But I believe that the previous, successful consultant has the right to be given the opportunity to show what she can do before you turn to another.

Again, it is a simple case of enlightened self-interest. The consultant who has satisfied you in the past has:

- ❑ Learned about your business: the way it is organized, what you are seeking to achieve and probably something of your internal politics. This knowledge takes time to build and time is literally money.

- ❏ Demonstrated that she can achieve the results you have specified within an acceptable timeframe. How will you know that a newcomer can do as much?
- ❏ Shown that she can work with your people to achieve results. She has demonstrated a capacity for both leadership (using personal and organizational power to get things done) and teamwork. Can you be sure that another consultant will not overemphasize one at the expense of the other?

If clients are disloyal to their satisfactory consultants then those consultants will be forced by the pressures of economic survival to take certain steps, none of which are in the client's interest – and none of which are acceptable, no matter how widely practiced, to those who take the profession seriously. To ensure an adequate flow of work she may either:

- ❏ accept more work than she can properly handle, reducing at the same time the quality of her outputs and her flexibility to deal with the unexpected
- ❏ create and sustain ongoing client dependence so that she will always be needed.

In order to stamp out these unnecessary practices, if you are responsible for hiring consultants in your organization, think very carefully and give repeat business to consultants who have already given you excellent service.

10

Fees and Contracts

'For two days labor you ask two hundred guineas?'
'No, I ask it for the experience of a lifetime.'
James McNeill Whistler

I BELIEVE THAT FEW THINGS A CONSULTANT COMMUNICATES TELL YOU more about her than the fees she charges. I am not saying the higher the better – were that the case I would not be writing this book! Some who charge the highest fees are worth every cent, but not all.

Low fees, on the other hand, may mean one of the following:

❑ The consultant does not need the money. Some of the best academics in their field charge surprisingly low fees on those rare occasions when they are available.
❑ She has little business sense and fails to realize that her fee is the only thing which will pay her salary, meet the expenses of doing business and enable her business to grow.

- ❑ She is neither very good, nor very confident in her own ability.
- ❑ She is being mainly financed by some government handout.

What is important is not the size of the fee but how it has been established. Before going into this in a little detail, let me remind you when the matter of the fee ought to start warning bells ringing in your ears.

If the consultant appears to be flying a kite and trying to see what she can get away with by way of a fee, retreating if you challenge the high price and offering to do the job for less, she is probably both dishonest and incompetent. Consultancy demands mutual trust. It is difficult to trust someone who tried to screw more out of you than the job is shown to be worth.

The laws of classical economics do not apply to the provision of professional services any more than they apply to the demand for high-ticket items and luxury goods. John Harvey-Jones, Tom Peters or Chris Prahalad turn away more work than they ever lose because their fees are high. The important thing is that the fee reflects the ability and value of the consultant, not the power of the market.

If 'everything is negotiable' it is a dead giveaway. These people and their clients know the price of everything and the value of nothing. The only reason for using an external consultant is to gain significant added value. Do you really believe that quibbling over a cent here or a centime there is going to add to the value you receive? Added value is an optional extra which is in the gift of the professional. Similar, but even worse, is the 'what can you afford? I'll take it' approach. A professional's fees are not negotiable. Let me explain why.

An independent consultant's fee is made up of three elements:

Fees and Contracts

- the consultant's salary
- coverage of overheads
- a sufficient profit so that, in the words of Peter Drucker, the business can perpetuate itself and grow.

The expenses of completing the assignment are independent of the overheads of running the business and should always be itemized and charged for separately. If they are included in the fee it is a clear sign either that the consultant is an amateur, or that she is working on some government scheme and bound by rules dreamed up by a bureaucrat who would not recognize a business if it were to run up and bite his ankles.

Any competent businessperson seeks to reduce uncertainty – bundling expenses into the total price always increases uncertainty. There is always the possibility of needing to make unexpected visits to distant plants with unanticipated stays at expensive hotels. If the consultant fails to charge for these the assignment may become uneconomic and savings may be surreptitiously made elsewhere, often to such a degree that the whole project is marred.

If, conversely, the unexpected is guessed at and allowed for, you will almost certainly find yourself being charged more than is necessary or appropriate within an inflated daily rate. Either way you, the client, suffer.

Setting the fee

Let us look briefly at how the professional sets her fees. She will first establish her salary expectations. This will be a realistic assessment of what someone with her skills, knowledge and experience might be expected to earn were she to take a real job. If she is an operational consultant – in effect a pair of extra, highly skilled hands – this may be a simple matter of looking at the recruitment ads, or considering what she is offered by those who seek to attract her to join their team.

If, on the other hand, she is an advisory consultant offering unique insights and experience, assessing her income potential will be a little more difficult. By comparing her own abilities and outcomes with those of her peers, by discussing the value she delivers with trusted clients and by searching out those with similar skills who prefer to be employed, she will find out what she needs to know.

The salary element, by the way, is pure salary; perks, if any, are overheads. Assuming that most of us who earn wages are paid for five days a week every week and also for vacations and public holidays, our consultant will need to cover her annual salary in 261 days' work. So her annual salary divided by 261 (365 days minus 104 weekend days) becomes her 'labor rate'.

Happy would be the consultant who was able to work on client business and invoice her efforts 261 days each year, but sadly, such a work rate is not possible even for the best of us. Therefore the consultant will estimate the number of days when she is confident of being involved in 'drilling, filling and billing'. The shortfall represented by the remaining days becomes an overhead of doing business, as she uses the time for marketing, administration, selling, self-development and all the myriad activities which the self-employed need to do to keep their heads above water.

So, if her best estimate of the number of days that she will be involved in billable work is 141 (note how easy she makes the arithmetic for me!) she will have 120 days, 10 days a month, which must form part of her overheads. Assuming a salary of $100,000, she will have a daily labor rate of $383 a day (100,000/261) and for 10 days each month she will need

Fees and Contracts

to recover this as part of her overhead.

Overheads are what you would expect them to be. They will include rent for her office, leasing or buying her car and computer, health and professional insurance, her training and development, stationery and postage and the other costs which enable each of us to stay in business. She will estimate these over a year and divide the annual total by the number of days for which she plans to bill her clients (141). In this way she ensures, as far as she can, that all overheads are properly recovered and that, although the clients pay for everything, they pay for nothing which is not a justifiable cost of doing business.

Assuming that her overheads are $141,000, working 141 days a year she will need to recover $1000 each billable day. So her labor rate and overhead recovery combined will total $1383 a day.

Faced with a daily rate of $1383, many will simply round this up to $1400 and assume that will provide a reasonable level of profit. Others, more financially astute perhaps, will consider their strategy, calculate the level of investment required to grow at the rate planned and use an accurate level of profit which will enable such growth to take place.

I am not pretending that it is necessarily appropriate for you to ask for a detailed breakdown of how the daily rate is split between salary, overhead and profit – any more than I would expect the consultant to ask you what you earn before advising you of what she proposes to charge you. But, if you want to know whether your potential consultant is a business professional rather than a handwaver, you would be well advised to ask something along the lines of: 'I obviously don't want to stick my nose into your private affairs, but would you mind telling me how you arrive at your daily fee rate?' If the consultant appears to be confused or upset by such a question, you can draw your own conclusions.

The way in which a large consultancy establishes its fees is similar. Salaries must be paid, including the seven-figure salaries at the top; overheads, including the cost of bringing together the cutting edge of business information, must be met; and since few would understand the value of growth better than they, the need to make a profit relevant to their investment plans will be incorporated.

Just to give you a ballpark idea of what it takes to meet the justifiable needs of a consulting leviathan these days, the *Economist* published some figures a couple of years ago which gave me food for thought. In the giants of consultancy each employee brought in average revenues, in round figures, as follows:

McKinsey and Co.	$469,000
Booz-Allen & Hamilton	$209,000
Ernst & Young	$149,000
Deloitte-Touche Tohmatsu	$144,000
Coopers & Lybrand	$142,000
Andersen Consulting	$125,000

In case you are worried that some, like Andersen, are barely scraping by, let me reassure you. Andersen Consulting has earned growth of almost 30 percent a year for several years now. In 1997 estimated growth in the industry was around 27 percent with some, such as Coopers & Lybrand, enjoying 32 percent more business than they did the previous year.

Consultancy has been a high-growth business for decades and shows every sign of continuing to experience sustained high growth. The Management Consultants' Association (the trade association of medium to large consultancies) made it clear in a public statement in early 1998 that its concern was not shortage of business – it is the growing difficulty of finding fully qualified people to do the vast amount of work available.

What about retainers?

What does the way in which consultants approach retainers tell the astute client?

Consultants love retainers. A retainer puts money in the bank, bread on the table and makes a contribution to paying the mortgage in the predictable way that bank managers and spouses love to see. But not all retainers are the same.

Suppose you approach me and tell me that on the second Monday and Tuesday of each month for the next year you wish to have exclusive use of my services. On these days I am to meet you and we will evaluate progress towards the achievement of your dominance strategy, identifying and implementing corrective action in the face of emergent changes in the global economic and business environment.

I am delighted – not only am I able to block off 24 days in my diary which I no longer need to sell, but I know how much preparation I am likely to need to do for our meetings which are guaranteed to take place by the terms of our agreement. In fact, I am so delighted that I may, unless the preparation is particularly onerous, do the almost unthinkable and charge you less than my daily rate. Why? Simply because I do not have to expend cash or effort selling those days. They are certain business in an uncertain world in which marketing and selling my time is probably my major overhead. For this you will get a discount and added value beyond your wildest expectations.

You are, however, the ideal client. Others are less reliable. For example, another client suggests a retainer agreement.

Again I am pleased, but knowing this client I am less than delighted. He suggests that I make myself potentially available for a couple of days a month which he cannot specify and may not use. In some months he may need my services for more than a couple of days, but in other months he may need me not at all. He probably expects a discount and, in a way, he is going to get one, but I need to educate him, or at least remind him of the ways of the world. In the retainer which he would like:

- I am going to make myself available with no guarantee that my services will be used.
- I must be very careful not to fill my diary because I am bound by honor as well as a contract to ensure that I have enough flexibility to meet with him at short notice.
- If he chooses not to use my services at all in any month I have lost the ability to sell that time elsewhere. I will not waste it: I might read – or even write – a good business book. I might develop a new marketing approach. I might do many things including decorating my office, but what I cannot do is what I am in business to do, which is to sell my time to clients.

So what kind of 'discount' will I offer this client? The deal will be something like this:

- For the number of days on which he expects me to make myself available, I will charge half of my normal daily rate.
- On those days when he chooses to use my services I will charge, in addition, my full daily rate. To make this absolutely clear, I charge 50 percent of my normal fee for being available but ignored and 150 per cent when my services are used.

Fees and Contracts

- Days not taken up in one month cannot be carried forward into the next. I charge for my availability.

Let me explain in a little more detail. Making myself available without any certainty that I shall be used involves me in an 'opportunity cost'. Not only must I turn down some assignments because they would be a barrier to being available, but I cannot sell unused days, so if I am not used I lose out twice. Having already lost the opportunity to do business at what is, after all, a carefully assessed and fair price, I cannot afford, and would not be prepared, to give anything further away. To go from losing potentially half my fee to throwing all of it away would be insane. For these reasons I am compensated somewhat for my loss of earning opportunity when I work for this client by receiving more than my normal daily rate. Similarly, he cannot expect to be able to carry forward unused time for the very simple reason that he has not paid for it. He has paid only for me to be available and that I have delivered.

I say 'I have delivered', but this is purely hypothetical. Personally I would never accept such a vague retainer, but consultancies with a sufficient number of staff often will. Their conditions for acceptance probably are, or ought to be:

- The person available and doing the work may not be the principal, but will be a properly qualified member of staff.
- The cost to the client (50 percent and 150 percent) will be as explained above for the same reasons.
- If the client wishes to specify who will do the work, they must specify the days on which they wish it to be done and pay the full fixed day retainer price.
- Unused time cannot, in any circumstances, be carried forward. It is the consultant's responsibility to be available as agreed. It is the client's responsibility to make the best possible use of that availability.

Performance contracts

No really competent and self-confident consultant should ever be afraid of being paid on the basis of the results that they achieve, which is what a performance contract involves. She may, however, need to explain very carefully how such a contract works.

Some time ago I was peripherally involved with a group of family-owned car dealerships. It was facing a problem: the service department of the group's flagship dealership was losing money. Those who know the automotive trade will be aware that, in theory at least, it is difficult and should be impossible to lose money in a franchised automotive service operation. In somewhat simplified terms, service labor is paid about one third of what it costs, so the gross profit is around 66 percent. If labor is managed effectively it is unlikely that a busy service department can carry enough costs to eat up such a gross profit.

Faced with the problem of mounting service losses in an otherwise profitable business, the company decided to employ a new service manager. It sought and found an experienced man (I'm not being sexist, they would not have considered hiring a woman even if they could have found one) with a reputation for solving problems, speaking his mind and making profits better than the industry average. The company was delighted when he asked for a relatively modest salary. He also insisted on a bonus of 10 percent of his departmental profits. Within a matter of weeks he had implemented changes which had the department running smoothly and profitably.

Month by month as the departmental profit figures emerged there was a minor celebration in the boardroom. The profits went from being non-existent, through highly gratifying to dramatic. New profitable business was being attracted, kept

Fees and Contracts   135

and efficiently serviced week by week. On the basis of its afterservice the reputation of the dealership soared. Everyone was happy until the end of the year.

By this time departmental profits were the model for the industry and still growing. The finance director worked out what was owed to the service manager and swallowed hard. Although his salary remained modest, the bonus to which he was entitled would make him the highest paid executive in the business. His total earnings would considerably exceed those of the chairman and in the company's view this could not be allowed to happen.

So, rather than 10 percent of the service profit, they offered 5 percent of the profit for the whole dealership. The service manager promptly rejected their kind offer on the grounds that his department's contribution was considerably greater than half the total, that he would only be paid on what he could manage and that they had an agreement on the basis of which he had accepted the job.

The company made other seductive offers – the title of deputy managing director, a bigger and better company car – but all to no avail. In the end they grudgingly paid what was owed and began to manufacture a case to force someone whose success was so embarrassing out of the business. It took a while, but eventually they managed it.

Indeed, had they managed it a little earlier they might have avoided a case for unfair dismissal which cost them a considerable amount of compensation and bad publicity. But to them it was a minor triumph. 'No one should earn more than the chairman' had become their credo to which they still clung when, a couple of years later, the department began to haemorrhage money again.

This is often the attitude of clients toward performance contracts. Never mind all the extra profit that we are now enjoying, we are not prepared to pass on even a relatively small percentage of it to the person who made it happen. No wonder the Pied Piper was less than happy with the burghers of Hamelin. Performance contracts are in everyone's interests, but only if they are properly managed.

The competent consultant, if payment by results is suggested, will make the following abundantly clear. This time she will put it into a legally binding contract which she will be untypically prepared to enforce.

- ❏ You will pay more, a very great deal more, than a straight fee: probably 30 percent of gains in year one, 25 percent of gains in year two and a final payment of 20 percent in year three. This could well run into millions if based on, say, a sales increase.
- ❏ The method of measurement will be predetermined and will be rigidly adhered to by your finance people. Creative accounting in these situations is so rife that when I work to a performance contract I tend to insist that I receive a copy of the VAT return each quarter and invoice what I am owed on the basis of the growth in the amount of turnover declared.
- ❏ She will not finance the assignment and will expect to be paid her normal daily rate or something close to it during the assignment, deducting payments from future claims.
- ❏ Normal terms and conditions for all payments will be observed.

Reading this you may be wondering why the possibility of suing a client has arisen and what has happened to trust. I tell you frankly that in every company there are people, corporate bureaucrats, who will do everything they can to avoid paying the firm's dues. Sadly, since what gets rewarded in a business is what gets done, these people are little less than an alibi for those above them. Why be ready to sue on this one occasion? Because if a business tends to try to wriggle out of its commitments the fact that it is unreliable is generally known throughout the industry. If a consultant works for such a company she is perceived to be a fool. If she lets them get away with it she is finished.

The contract

As well as agreeing a suitable fee, a knowledgeable consultant will always wish to draw up a contract for any assignment which extends beyond, say, one day. The contract will be as simple as possible and, although it is a legally enforceable document, no consultant worthy of the name would think of suing a client other than *in extremis*.

The purpose of the contract is to communicate clearly and succinctly to both parties:

- ✔ What the consultant has undertaken to do.
- ✔ What the client has agreed to contribute (information, clerical support etc.).
- ✔ When such support is needed to ensure that the assignment is completed on time to the quality agreed.
- ✔ Who owns the outcome. This is particularly important where, for example, a training program or software is developed during the project.
- ✔ The circumstances under which the client or the consultant can transfer the assignment, or any part of it, to a third party.
- ✔ How much the consultant is to be paid and, most important to the consultant, when the money will be in her bank account.

You may work in a corporation in which a legal department writes all the contracts. If you are hiring an effective consultant she will move heaven and earth not to be bound by such a contract. She will, at the very least, insist that it is carefully checked and amended for the following reasons:

- ❑ The average contract written by a lawyer obfuscates rather than facilitates clear communication.
- ❑ It is unlikely that a contract written in a company legal department will put any responsibility of any kind on the company. Consultancy is mutual problem solving where if you fail to do your part I cannot hope to do mine.

Lawyers may try to write into a contract a requirement which binds the consultant to perform something which it is simply not in her power to do. Where, for example, you are seeking ISO 9000 or similar accreditation, the consultant can prepare the required documentation to the level necessary and do it by the agreed date. She cannot control the behavior of third-party accreditors who may, on a whim it seems, choose to be easy or difficult to satisfy. A consultant cannot, therefore, undertake to get you the accreditation by the date you hope for. To sign a contract which demands it would be an act of idiocy or ignorance.

So if your consultant is loathe to provide a simple contract or is too quick to sign the standard form thrown out in great number by your industrious legal department, take care. She may not be operating in the real world.

Sample contract

As the above makes clear, I believe that the purpose of the contract is to facilitate communication, not to provide a legal basis for the assignment. When expectations are both clear and predetermined, a context is created in which legal enforcement is neither necessary nor desirable.

A consultancy contract which exceeds a single sheet of paper is almost certainly counterproductive. With the possible exception noted subsequently, the sample contract on page 140 should be more than adequate.

If a performance contract were involved, a slightly more complex agreement would be advisable. An example begins on page 141.

ABC Consultancy Inc., 123 New Road, Anytown, AB 10010

2 January 1999

AGREEMENT

The Assignment

ABC Consultancy Inc. undertakes to design, develop and conduct a training program, 'The Psychology of Leadership', with the pilot session taking place on or before 1 April 1999 for the board of directors of Megabucks Corporation Inc. Necessary revisions will be completed and the full program will be rolled out by 1 May 1999. Two programs will be conducted per month (excluding August) May through December 1999. Megabucks Corporation will ensure that a minimum of twelve and a maximum of sixteen executives will attend each course and will administer attendance. ABC will provide all necessary course documentation and will conduct participant evaluations of each program within twelve weeks of delivery.

Intellectual Property

The program will remain the intellectual property of ABC Consultancy Inc. and will be conducted by a principal consultant or by a guest speaker previously authorized by Megabucks Corporation Inc.

Payment

Megabucks Corporation Inc. will pay $12,000 for each two-day program. Payment terms are fourteen days from date of invoice.

In addition, Megabucks Corporation Inc. will pay $25,000 on signing of this agreement as a part payment towards the design and development of the program.

Transferability

This agreement, once entered into, is not transferable by either party without the full and express agreement of the other.

Signed .... (for Megabucks Corporation Inc.) Date ....
Signed .... (for ABC Consulting Inc.)   Date ....

ABC Consultancy Inc., 123 New Road, Anytown, AB 10010

2 January 1999

AGREEMENT

The Assignment

ABC Consultancy Inc. will design, develop and conduct for Megabucks Corporation Inc. a sales training program, 'The Power of Influence'. This program will be fully supported by a coaching and mentoring program incorporating peer and supervisor coaching which will be project managed by senior members of the ABC Consultancy Inc. senior team. The program will lead to an increase in sales revenues as measured by Megabucks Corporation's independent auditors of not less than fifty per cent by 31 December 2000.

The program will initially be conducted as follows:

1 May to 30 June 1999
A pilot group (Team 'A'), constituted of a randomly selected one-third of the sales team, will experience the full training and coaching program.

A second group (Team 'B'), of the same size and also randomly selected, will be given an additional sales incentive of five per cent from 1 July 1999.

A third group (Team 'C'), made up of the balance of the sales team, will experience no changes to their work conditions or remuneration.

1 July to 30 September 1999
Measurement of each team's sales performance will be carried out by Megabucks Corporation's independent auditor and the results made available to ABC Consultancy Inc. by 15 October 1999.

When comparison of the three teams' sales performance has clearly demonstrated the superiority of the training program as a means of sustainable sales improvement, the program will be scheduled for attendance by all members of the sales team by 30 December 1999.

16 October to 31 December 1999
An accelerated program of training will be completed to ensure that all members of teams 'B' and 'C' undergo training and coaching by 31

December 1999. Megabucks Corporation Inc. will administer participation to ensure attendance in groups of between 16 and 20 participants for each scheduled course.

1 January 2000 to 31 December 2000
Megabucks Corporation Inc.'s independent auditors will measure Megabucks Corporation's sales revenues and the results will be made available to ABC Consultancy Inc. by 15 February 2001.

Payment Schedule
1. Program design
An advance of $25,000 is payable on signing of this agreement.

2. Program implementation
Megabucks Corporation Inc. will pay $6000 per consultant/day to ABC Consultancy Inc. for training and post-program coaching throughout the period of the program.

3. Success fees
ABC Consultancy Inc. will be paid five percent of the value of increased sales revenues during the year commencing 1 January 2000 when compared with the previous year (less payments already made at the per diem rate). This will be based on the published and audited accounts and will be paid in full not later than 31 March 2001.

Intellectual Property
The program will remain the intellectual property of ABC Consultancy Inc. and will be offered to client organizations entirely at the discretion of ABC Consultancy Inc.

Transferability
This agreement is not transferable by either party, but may be concluded by mutual consent if the sales performance of Team 'A' in the period 30 June to 30 September 1999 fails to exceed those of the other teams.

Signed .... (for Megabucks Corporation Inc.) Date ....
Signed .... (for ABC Consulting Inc.)   Date ....

What is a day?

Occasionally clients ask me what a day is. I charge by the day, so they have the right to ask. For me, and for most good consultants, it is a normal working day of, say, eight hours. If the client is prepared to work longer than eight hours – and work meaningfully on the project, not simply hang around – I will work happily alongside him at no extra charge.

If, however, the client expects me to work 18 hours a day for an eight-hour stipend while he goes home and immerses himself in the intellectual glories of television, he is mistaken. I will work exceptional hours when the job requires it, but the decision to do so is solely mine. The client gets his pound of flesh and a great deal more during the normal working day. If he wants more he has to show that he is prepared to sweat by my side.

So if you want to evaluate a consultant's timekeeping you can have no better yardstick than your own.

The matter of payment

As I commented in the discussion of performance contracts, no competent consultant would ever knowingly work for a company which does not pay its bills and pay them on time. To do so not only damages the consultant's cashflow, it also damages her reputation.

The contract will be explicit on when payment is to be made and make it clear that 'paid' means that the money has been cleared and is in the consultant's bank account on the specified date. It does not mean that the finance director will start the long process which leads to a check being issued only on the day the cash is due.

The terms and conditions of doing business which accompany the proposal will reinforce the payment expectations.

The intelligent consultant will ask for money up front wherever this can be justified. Many assignments carry heavy costs at the front end and there is no reason for the consultant to want to finance activities which are solely in the interest of the client even for a short time.

She will also try to plan her work so that the due date for some major deliverable and payment coincide. Without being unpleasant or aggressive about it, the deliverable will be late if and only if the check is late.

The streetwise consultant will immediately make you aware that she has not received payment and will stop work until the check is at least in her hands, if not in her bank. She will also ask her bank manager to arrange for express clearance.

If all of the above fails she will walk away from the contract, retaining against payment all information or other deliverables available at that time. If this extreme step becomes necessary she will not pick up the assignment again after payment unless the reasons for non-payment are in some way unique.

We had a recent situation in which we asked for a modicum of payment up front, but since the matter was urgent we began work before the check arrived, assuming that what had been promised would be delivered. The check is now two months late. We have information which has a value to the client many times what is owed to us. What is more, we are very close to being able to deliver to the client everything he desires and more.

I have today written withdrawing from the assignment, offering to send to the client the information we have collected, but making it clear that after this breach of trust we cannot act further on his behalf. This is sad, but it is business and a good consultant serves no one well by being other than businesslike.

Fees and Contracts

Too often the assumption is made that the vendor needs the buyer more than the buyer needs the vendor. In the world of consultancy this is no longer true, even for the one-person outfit as long as she is competent. There is a shortage of good consultants and in most cases the client is buying in a seller's market. The consultant cannot afford, and never agrees, to become the client's alternative to an overdraft.

May I ask you to consider what may appear to be an impertinent question: if your finance department owed you a substantial sum of money and, in spite of an agreement, showed little sign of paying, how long would you be prepared to wait?

11

The Consulting Process

People aren't necessarily right because they are being paid twice or even ten times as much as you are.

Ros Miles

WHETHER YOU BUY IN CONSULTANCY OR DEVELOP YOUR OWN internal capacity, you need to be able to manage the consulting process. The range of tools is too wide to provide in less than another book (*Key Management Solutions* is a useful source of tools and techniques). However, to ensure high value consulting you need to be aware of the key stages in the process and what the consultant should be doing in each. More details on individual stages are found throughout the current book.

If you are using external consultants, you will have the capability to blend their activities with what can be provided internally to improve the quality of outcomes and save money. If you develop and use an internal consultancy capability, the same understanding will enable you to be sure that your team performs to the high standards that you will rightly demand of outsiders.

Some of the detail of the stages will be different for internal and external consultants, but this is only a matter of emphasis. The internal consultant should be, at all times, equally professional and equally thorough.

The consulting process

Stage one: Marketing and public relations

The qualified consultant works consistently to bring her skills to the notice of her prospective clients by indulging in highly professional marketing activities. She takes every reasonable advantage of opportunities for good press coverage and keeps the media informed of newsworthy stories, awards that she receives, professional accreditation and, if she is a writer, books published. She builds, through performance not hype, her personal business status and reputation.

Stage two: Client inquiry or request to serve

The consultant visits the potential client and assesses both his need and her ability to serve. She will try to establish any limits on the client's power to act and whether any organizational politics or other factors will affect her ability to serve to the highest professional standards. Understanding that the client is a person with whom she will need to work closely, she will seek evidence that they will be a good team.

Stage three: The proposal

Good consultants write proposals for all extended interventions whether or not the client wants to see them. In essence, the proposal should tell both the consultant and the client:

- the outcome to be achieved
- the key activities which must be performed to achieve the desired outcome
- the value to the client of performing each of these activities
- how long the intervention will take
- what it will cost.

Stage four: The contract

The contract will say:

- what is to be done
- how much and with what frequency the consultant is to be paid
- what the client has agreed to provide
- who owns products, if any, which result from the intervention
- how much time the consultant will devote to the client organization
- the circumstances under which the consultant may introduce colleagues into the client organization
- the circumstances under which the client is free to cancel the contract and engage an alternative consultant.

The contract should be seen as more of an exercise in good communication than as a legal agreement to be enforced. It is, in a very real sense, a contract of honor and it should be a model of clarity and simplicity.

Stage five: Performance

The consultant performs the key activities and provides regular briefing, feedback and monitoring opportunities to the client. She manages her time effectively to ensure that she meets all deadlines in spite of the occasional unforeseen problems which will arise.

Stage six: Withdrawal

The consultant completes the project, ensures that the client is delighted with the outcome and is able to act without help in similar situations in the future. The delighted client may provide business referrals to the consultant.

The intervention

The above is a skeletal summary of what happens. For practical purposes we need to look at the intervention and what happens immediately before it in greater detail.

Pre-entry

The consultant clearly establishes who the client is and his position in the formal and informal business hierarchy. She also clarifies the areas of the business in which she must work and the key opinion leaders, in addition to her client, whom she must satisfy.

She will also make sure that she understands the client organization's important products and services and will attempt, if she is not already a specialist, to begin to fast-track her understanding of the industry and the markets in which it operates.

She will consider her own behavior and attitudes and assess how easy it will be for her to work with the client on a personal basis. If necessary she will consider how she may need to adjust her own behavior to facilitate the relationship.

The consultant will build a tentative theory of the organization's overall situation and identify ways in which she may test this theory at the earliest possible moment to avoid working on unfounded assumptions. She will do the same in respect of the client company's sector. Above all, she will seek to establish that she fully understands the key issues facing the client and his industry.

If any 'no go' areas have been identified by the client, the consultant will attempt to establish what effect this may have on her ability to deliver the desired results on time.

Finally, she will try to establish what information, external to the client organization, she will need early in the intervention and where it may be obtained quickly.

Entry

The consultant will ensure above all that she fully understands the client's desired outcome and will seek to convince herself that her approach, including her personal style, is likely to achieve that outcome within the client's timeframe.

She will make the essential early contacts which will facilitate her performance of the assignment.

Data collection

The consultant will collect all data relevant to her assignment. She will not ask for information she does not need. If anything additional comes her way which might be important, she will pass it on to her client during her regular briefing sessions or prior to them if the matter appears to be urgent.

A key part of the data which will be relevant at this stage may be the degree to which the organization is ready for change. A number of excellent, well-established tests exist which will enable the consultant to quantify the situation and predict potential problems. Avoidance and contingency plans will be discussed with the client and implemented with his agreement.

All data will be summarized and fully discussed with the client.

Intervention

The consultant will complete the activities indicated by the timetable in her proposal or as amended with the agreement of the client. She will work with key internal people nominated by her client and will ensure that after the intervention those who need to be are properly prepared to continue the initiative and take it forward. At all stages the consultant will keep the client fully informed of results and ensure his ongoing satisfaction.

Withdrawal

Having achieved the desired outcome and ensured that there will be no ongoing client dependence on the consultant, she will undertake the final debriefing. This has two main aims:

- to ensure the delight of the client and ascertain that she has omitted nothing which would have increased his satisfaction with the outcome
- to learn from the experience and plan her own future development.

The final debriefing will therefore be a thorough, detailed and wide-ranging discussion. The consultant will wish to discuss with you, in considerable detail, the areas outlined in the checklist on the next two pages.

Only if you show yourself to be delighted and excited by what has been achieved and determined to take it forward is the real professional satisfied with her performance. Only when she has a delighted client, keen to build on what has been achieved, confident about the way what has been done is accepted in the organization and anxious to find some ways of continuing the association will she be satisfied.

- ✔ Are you absolutely delighted with the outcome of her intervention?
- ✔ Is it precisely what you had planned for, or perhaps even better than you might have hoped?
- ✔ Can you think of anything, no matter how minor, that could have been done which was omitted?
- ✔ Is it apparent throughout the organization that it has been significantly helped?
- ✔ Are there any divisions or departments which feel that they might have lost out and, if so, is there anything which the consultant can do to help resolve any problem or protect you from any hassle?
- ✔ Are there any key individuals who feel they have lost out through the intervention and do you need help to address their concerns?
- ✔ Are members of your team demonstrably more able to deal with similar problems or opportunities which might arise in the future?
- ✔ Are they using their new knowledge and skills on a day-to-day basis to the benefit of the business?
- ✔ If not, are the steps which are being taken to maintain their new skills and their motivation to use them sufficient in your view?
- ✔ Does the organization have a new look, a new feel and a new way of approaching problems and opportunities?
- ✔ Does the organization have a better understanding of itself than before the intervention?
- ✔ Is the organization as a whole comfortable with its new knowledge?
- ✔ Has the consultant been entirely successful in avoiding the creation of problems elsewhere in the business? If, for example, a marketing plan has led to an unusually large contract, are you happy that the finance director is not losing sleep at night while he worries about where the extra working capital will come from, or how the early cashflow shortfall will be communicated to the bank?

- ✔ Is there anything in the consultant's approach or behavior which you would want her to change were she to work in your organization again?
- ✔ Do you feel that she could help again, in other ways?
- ✔ Is she likely to be invited back into the organization?
- ✔ Would you be comfortable referring her to others?
- ✔ How would you prefer her to stay in touch with you: regular brief telephone calls, her company newsletter, an occasional personal visit when in the area?
- ✔ Could you recommend any personal development or training which would make her of greater value to clients similar to yourself?
- ✔ Is there anything that she could do now to make you even more delighted with the outcome?

Announcing an internal consultancy service

If you take the option of developing your own internal consultancy team, an important part of the process will be to announce this to the rest of the organization.

If possible, make the announcement in conjunction with some major initiative. In this way you are able to show the reasoning behind creating the team. Managers and workers are often equally vocal in complaining about plans which they feel are thrust on them. What is more, since change generates further change much too quickly in most organizations there is a growing feeling that change is introduced for its own sake. So those who believe that they have enough to do coping with the familiar make little if any effort to make the new initiative work.

By announcing simultaneously that you are introducing a major change and providing qualified facilitators to help make it happen, you are showing that this time it really is different. This time the change is supported and important.

Part of my job is to kickstart failed initiatives. When I am trying to find out what went wrong four factors always emerge:

- change piled on change
- an attitude from management of 'cope dammit!'
- insufficient help to introduce changes effectively
- lack of training.

Just as with external advisers, there is a need to build the perceived status and credibility of the internal consultancy team quickly. This means that you need to market to your customers – directors, executives, managers, supervisors and workforce – with as much consistency and skill as the most successful external consultants apply in the global marketplace.

Marketing the team

In general terms you have an advantage over external consultants: your customers' needs are a given. If the change is inevitable they need to implement it with the minimum of disruption to their daily activities. So you should demonstrate clearly that establishing an internal consultancy team is the best means to achieve a hassle-free transition from where you are to where you need to be. You also need to demonstrate, and this should never be forgotten, that individually each member of the team has a unique and important contribution to make.

The first thing you must do is give the team an identity. It needs a name so it is identifiable as a meaningful entity. For the sake of avoiding cynicism, try to avoid anything too macho or overdramatic. If you have given your initiative a name, and you should, it is probably going to be enough to call the internal consultancy team the Operation Whatever Support Taskforce. It is essential to use a word like 'support' because not doing so will give the impression that the initiative and responsibility for making it happen is no longer with management, but with this new group.

The next stage is to start promoting the credibility of the individual members and, through them, the group. If you have selected your people with care and had them properly trained, then you have potentially good consultants. Our concern at the moment is to get those good consultants used.

The next few sections explain a range of proven, effective ways used in the tough competitive world of international consultancy to build reputation, credibility and business. The various activities have in common only that they cost little or nothing to do and that they have been proved to work in the toughest of competitive environments. Do not let their low cost seduce you into giving all of them a try and not giving any of them time to work. Treat them as a menu – select and combine options in the way that suits you best.

For the sake of simplicity the discussion is aimed at the internal consultants themselves. Most of the suggestions are of course equally applicable to external consultants who need to market themselves.

Giving talks to audiences of potential clients

The first thing is to avoid trying to sell your services. If you have been given the opportunity to speak you have been given a chance to help lift the black cloud of boredom, not to add to it. Few things are more boring than having people say, in effect, 'We know nothing of your particular circumstances, but we think so well of ourselves that we are sure you ought to be queuing in droves to use us. We have these wonderful individuals with these glorious and almost unattainable levels of skill and even if we've failed to convince you we have the backing of top management – so there.'

What you will do is different. You will think carefully and deeply about real problems which the members of your audience face: lack of time, lack of people, opposition to change in general and so on. You will then, with the help of your colleagues, find some simple but useful tools to overcome the key problem. You will present those tools by talking about, in this order:

- ✔ What it is that your audience wants to achieve. *(Someone cares about us for a change...)*
- ✔ What they are up against in trying to achieve it. *(This speaker understands.)*
- ✔ What they will gain by doing no more than listening to what you have to say. *(There could be something in this for me.)*
- ✔ What the tool is, how it works, why it will work for them, help and support that you can provide, what other support materials are available, who else has used the tool and how it has helped them. *(I could do that – perhaps with a little help.)*

Then summarize the benefits to them of using the tool, not in random order but in logical sequence so that each benefit in turn is clearly the logical consequence of its predecessor. The last benefit is the biggest of all: their objective which you specified at the beginning of your talk.

Do this and they will be desperate to talk to you at the end of the meeting. Do anything by way of a direct sale and they will go back to their offices and departments as fast as they can get away.

To build on a good beginning you must do one more thing. You must give them something on paper which reinforces what you have said. A step-by-step guide on how to apply the tool would be ideal. This handout also needs to carry your, or your group's, extension number and an invitation to use it for further information and other problem-solving ideas.

Ideally it will not be on a flat sheet of A4, or worse on a number of sheets. It could be on a small card, folded if necessary to provide four sides, which they can keep at hand on their desks. Or, if the budget will not run to printed cards, you could use a piece of paper, 'z' folded so that it will conveniently go into a pocket or purse, but not into a file where it may be forgotten or impossible to retrieve.

You may choose to use the opportunity to promise, and deliver, some further helpful tips a few days after the meeting by way of your organization's intranet. This will act as a useful reminder that one person at least had something helpful to say, said it and shut up. That is how reputations are made.

Attending other people's meetings

You don't need to be the featured speaker to make an impression at meetings. If you attend as a member of the audience, sit near the front where you can be seen.

When it is relevant, ask a question or make a point which demonstrates that you understand and have sympathy with the other members of the audience and follow this with a brief comment: 'Your audience may find it useful to know that in doing internal consultancy we...' Now everybody knows that you are intelligent, helpful and a member of the new internal consultancy team that people are beginning to talk about.

Later if there is a refreshment break, stand where you are easily accessible in the middle of the room, look sociable, and people will approach you, their newly discovered friendly expert.

Seminars

The relationship that builds between a seminar leader and the participants is usually a warm one and giving seminars will rapidly build your reputation and status in the eyes of your potential market.

Of course, the subject of the seminar must be of interest, and you need not limit yourself to the initiative if your intent is, in the nicest way possible, self-promotion. In very general terms what people like to know about is:

- How to make more money.
- How to keep more of the money that they make.
- How to avoid hassle at work.
- How to live a richer life away from work.

If you can design and present a seminar which in some way relates to any of the above then you will have an audience. Your seminar must, of course, also make sense within the terms of their daily activities and the company strategy.

So you may, for example, develop a program showing how effective personalized handling of stress will literally make you younger. This would satisfy the 'avoiding hassle' and 'richer life' needs as well as enabling people to be more effective in day-to-day operations.

From the point of view of increasing your credibility as a partner in problem solving, it hardly matters what subject you choose as long as it is relevant and useful and it will attract an audience. Being seen as an 'authority' leads people to ask your advice concerning a whole range of problems, most of which have little or nothing to do with the content of the seminar. You have shown yourself to be an articulate and approachable authority, and that is enough.

It is possible that public speaking in any form fills you with terror, so can you write clearly and concisely? If so, there are considerable opportunities for you to build your reputation.

Articles

If you have a company magazine you may find that writing articles for it gets your name and your views well known throughout the organization. That helps, but it is doubtful whether being a published writer in such a domestic medium does a great deal for building your status unless you turn your column into something special. You could try to convince the editor that you, or you and your new colleagues, might produce a corporate agony column.

Of course, your reputation will flourish more quickly if your efforts are published somewhere a little more prestigious. This is easier than perhaps it sounds. Most trade and industry magazines and journals and most regional business magazines and newspapers are anxious for input. Send unsolicited articles to them with a note saying in effect 'first come first served, so let me know if you are going to print this' and, if your experience is anything like mine was a few years ago, you will get acceptances and invitations to write more.

Have a decent photograph taken by the company photographer and send a copy with the article and that alone will increase your chances of being published. Finally, send your submission to the editor by name and not by title.

After publication, get a number of reprints and send one through the internal mail to each decision maker. If possible, get your boss or your boss's boss to handwrite a brief note along the lines of: 'Have your people read this interesting article by...' If necessary write a note yourself: 'I thought this would be useful to you in case you missed it...' Either way, your article is likely to be read by the people who count, the prestigious publication will be noted and your reputation will soar.

Newsletters

Many consultants and most consultancies produce newsletters, and frankly they are wasting their time. This is not because newsletters do not build reputations and bring in assignments – they do – but because most consultant-produced newsletters are garbage publications full of self-congratulation and promotional puff. A single sheet with relevant, timely, practical and useful information, spiced up, if possible, with a little non-conformity, is worth far more.

Writing a book

The biggest, the best, the most effective way to build your personal credibility as a consultant is to write a book. If you have a burning desire to be an author nothing I can say will stop you, but let me try.

If you write an uncommissioned first book the chances are that it will:

❑ fail to attract the attention of a publisher
❑ if published, fail to sell.

That will not bother the committed 'wannabe' author, however, so, if you have a book in you, write it and be damned. But please ask someone in the book business, a publisher or, better in my opinion, a book retailer, whether it stands any chance of being published before you go too far.

If, on the other hand, you have already written a book and had it published, whether it sold or not, have your boss sign an order for enough copies to get one into the hands of every decision maker in the organization. They won't necessarily read it. Research shows that most of us, on average, reach page 26 of a non-fiction work before we give up and place the book on the shelf – but you will be a celebrity. A minor celebrity, but a celebrity nonetheless. As such, you will be listened to and your advice will be sought.

12

Maximizing the Benefit

Endless meetings, sloppy communications and red tape steal the entrepreneur's time.

James Hayes

CLIENTS ARE JUSTIFIABLY FRIGHTENED BY THE VISION OF consultants frenetically charging around the organization, doing God alone knows what. Fortunately, it is avoidable.

However, if you follow my advice when you seek and select a consultant you lay firm foundations for managing the intervention. You will have carefully considered your needs and established clear outcomes. You will also be aware of the details of the consulting process and what should be achieved at each stage.

In addition to this, at an early meeting with the consultant it is important to check her understanding of the outcome you require and gain her agreement not just that the outcome is possible, but that she can and will deliver it to you within an agreed timescale. At the same meeting write into your diary specific dates on which you will meet with your consultant to discuss progress.

Make it clear that these meetings are for you to be briefed on and evaluate progress, not for the consultant to pursue her own agenda. In short, he who is paying the piper is, very properly, calling the tune. There is more on these progress briefings later in the chapter.

Never forget that when you meet with your consultant you are paying for the privilege, and you may be paying several hundred dollars an hour. You have every right, therefore, to dictate the purpose, form and range of discussion.

This is not to say that the consultant is in any way constrained from telling you exactly and in detail what is happening – giving frank and unbiased advice remains her responsibility. It also remains her responsibility to tell you immediately if anything unexpected occurs or, indeed, if there is anything, directly relevant to the assignment or not, which you have a need to know. The consultant owes her loyalty directly to you as the person who hired her.

Please bear with me while I explain with an example what I mean. Suppose that you ask me into your organization to investigate a 'people problem'. For the sake of argument let us assume that morale, motivation and performance have all taken a nose dive.

Let us further assume, unlikely as it may sound, that my investigation shows that you, and you alone, are responsible. The conflict between your spoken philosophy and your actions is such that the workforce has lost all commitment to the goals of the business and simply goes through the motions with minimal expenditure of effort to remain in place to collect their wages and salaries. What am I, your consultant, to do?

Maximizing the Benefit

Some, and I believe their behavior to be totally unethical and motivated only by the need to continue to receive their fees, will approach the chairman or other board members like some latter-day Iago and recommend your removal. Others will confront you with the problem and tell you how you may change your behavior. The second behavior is closer, but not close enough, to what ought to be done.

Certainly you will need to change your behavior in some way if the outcome of high morale is to be achieved, but the question is: how do we most readily get you to change? The use of the word 'we' is intentional. You may not be fully aware of it, but we are still involved in mutual problem solving. With some people confrontation is the appropriate way, with others a more tactful approach is essential. I must continue, if at all possible, to be able to work with you and to facilitate your ability to work with me. I will therefore use every influencing skill to ease your change of behavior and see confrontation as a last resort.

And if I fail? Then I must lay all my cards face up on the table. You are paying me, among other things, for frank and unbiased advice. At this stage, therefore, I tell you exactly what you must do and I pull no punches.

If you refuse then I am finished – literally. I have no choice but to withdraw from the contract, if possible introducing a colleague who may be more skilled in persuasion. I am still bound by the strongest ethical ties to support that colleague's activities in whatever ways she requires. I am, in other words, bound to provide her or you with any information I have and am under an absolute obligation not to discuss the matter with anyone other than my successor. Only she can initiate such a discussion.

Only if I am unable to bring in a suitably qualified colleague and have withdrawn am I free to discuss the situation with your supervisor. This can only be done with your full knowledge and, if you are willing, in your presence.

I was horrified some years ago to read that the Institute of Management Consultants advised its members that there were times when going behind a client's back is 'unethical, but sometimes acceptable'. I hope it has withdrawn that advice, which was based on a case where a consultant had been denied information by his principal client, but believed that he could persuade the client's personal assistant to hand it over during her boss's absence at lunch. What is unethical is never acceptable in a professional relationship. If some are misled into believing that it is so the case for managing consultants on the job is even stronger.

So, although you have made a good start, you cannot relax.

The proposal

Many clients refuse the consultant's offer of a proposal in their enthusiasm to get on with the job. They see it as a waste of time when they are already committed. I ought to admit that if they say they don't want one, they don't get one. Why should I irritate them by insisting they have something they don't want?

However, I do have to put together a proposal as my personal route map. There is an example of the kind of proposal I would recommend on pages 169–72. Individual consultants will add to the 'bare bones' shown here in any way they wish. They may, if the proposal is complex, add an executive summary. They may add their values or mission statement. They may choose to tell you who will do the work and what their qualifications are. They will certainly add a summary of costs – or, if they are shy, 'a note of your investment', which is the same thing only usually more expensive.

PROPOSAL

Understanding of the Brief

Megabucks Inc. is intent on developing and implementing a strategic and tactical plan which will enable it to monopolize those markets where it has, or can develop, a dominant competitive advantage.

In order to ensure the success of such a strategy the company needs to:

1. Identify emergent and future customer needs and desires in all the markets that it serves.
2. Assess the relative present and future capability of competition in those markets.
3. Specify those customers who, if they were attracted to Megabucks, would severely damage competition if they were lost.
4. Identify those current customers of Megabucks who cost more to service than they deliver in profit.
5. Develop both strategic and tactical plans based on the above information.
6. Identify the skills and knowledge required at every level in the business to assure the success of such a plan.
7. Prioritize training needs to ensure an approach consistent with the concept of 'lifelong learning – just in time'.
8. Conduct training in accordance with the priorities using internal resources whenever possible.
9. Ensure the transfer of learning to the workplace by using the latest ideas in peer coaching.

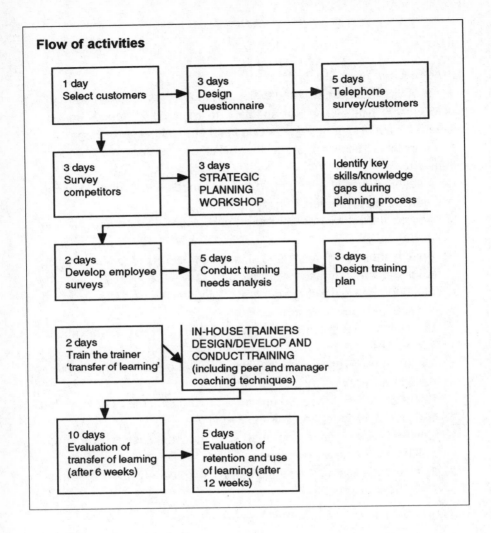

Benefit summary

Select customers
By analysing the cost of serving individual customers and the value of their business:
- ❑ The profile of the most desirable customer is established
- ❑ Emergent and future needs are focused on the most profitable sectors, segments and niches and identify the customers to be retained in each
- ❑ Unprofitable customers are identified and Megabucks can make a strategic decision which should continue to be served
- ❑ The most attractive customers currently served by competition are identified by type.

Design questionnaire
Development of a formal and scientific questionnaire ensures that:
- ❑ Customers perceive the activity as serious
- ❑ Answers are reliable
- ❑ Planning is based on valid and focused information.

Telephone survey
By using professional interviewing staff:
- ❑ Initial questions are strictly expressed according to questionnaire
- ❑ Supplementary questions are carefully applied
- ❑ Full information is gained
- ❑ Megabucks' status is enhanced in the eyes of important customers.

Survey competitors
- ❑ Competitor strengths and weaknesses are assessed in light of emergent customer needs and desires
- ❑ Vulnerable competitors are identified.

STRATEGIC PLANNING WORKSHOP
- ❑ The long-term growth potential and short-term profitability of the corporation are enhanced
- ❑ Competitors will be forced to lose money or withdraw from key markets...

Gantt chart of activities

　　　　Select
　　　　customers

　　　　　　Design
　　　　　　questions

　　　　　　　　Survey
　　　　　　　　customers

　　　　　　　　Survey
　　　　　　　　competitors

　　　　　　　　　　　PLANNING
　　　　　　　　　　　WORKSHOP

　　　　　　　　　　　　　Develop
　　　　　　　　　　　　　employee
　　　　　　　　　　　　　surveys

　　　　　　　　　　　　　　　Training
　　　　　　　　　　　　　　　needs
　　　　　　　　　　　　　　　analysis

　　　　　　　　　　　　　　　　　Design
　　　　　　　　　　　　　　　　　training
　　　　　　　　　　　　　　　　　plan

　　　　　　　　　　　　　　　　　　　Train the trainer

March 1　2–4　　7–11　　14–16　17–18　20–24　　27–28　29–30
　　　　　　　　　　　　　　Time line

Note: Your trainers will be able to design, develop and conduct training programs from 1 April and evaluation can start within six weeks of the first course. If the coaching and mentoring implementation is succeeding after six weeks and if learning is being applied effectively after 12 weeks, further evaluation may safely be left in the hands of Megabucks management.

Two important parts of a practical proposal are a flow chart and a Gantt chart.

I use the flow chart to prove to myself that the job can be done. Starting at the wrong end, the outcome, I chart activities back to where we are today. The Gantt chart shows the time that the assignment will take. I can show what activities overlap or can be done simultaneously so I can find the shortest path to completion. I can also use the Gantt chart to show where information or help from the client must be available. That way I can remind him in good time.

Think for a moment what you as a client can do with those two simple pieces of paper. You can check that I am doing only what I ought to be doing, that I have not gone merrily off on a tangent, and you can ascertain whether I am on track to finish the job to schedule.

You may want a flow chart and Gantt chart to be included as part of the contract. The contract is a means of communication rather than a sterile legal document, so even if your consultant is providing it, why don't you think about what you might like to communicate? You may, for example, add a short paragraph such as:

> *During the period of the assignment the consultant(s) will devote a minimum of x hours a month to the corporation's interests. Should this prove difficult in any month the consultant(s) shall seek the agreement of the corporation to vary the hours.*

If you are kind you may wish to add that permission to vary the hours will not be unreasonably refused. A simple sentence or two will reinforce your use of the Gantt chart by reminding you how often and for what periods the consultant has undertaken to be at your premises or working in your interests.

Where the work is done

If you have chosen the right consultant you need not worry when she is working on your behalf away from your premises. However, if you have any reason to doubt the consultant's reliability – if you believe that, given half a chance, she will slope off and play golf (charging you for her time) – you may wish to organize things so that most if not all of the work can be done at your premises. If you want to have the consultant constantly under your eye you may need to provide a suitable office, Internet access, secretarial support and other expensive things. But then it could be said that you made a mistake in appointing a consultant you can't trust, and in business the wages of sin have always been increased costs.

Progress briefings

As I said at the beginning of the chapter, it is important to agree on 'observable milestones' at weekly or biweekly intervals which will act as key indicators of progress towards the set goal. For example, if you want your sales team to be psychometrically assessed and subsequently trained, you might agree that by the end of week two the test will have been identified and bought in and by week three it will have been administered to a sample group of one-third of the sales team. This will be absolutely clear if the consultant has produced a proposal along the lines that I suggest, including a flow chart and Gantt chart; less so, perhaps, if they create an impressive bound book full of words and enthusiasm.

You now know exactly what you expect to hear at the briefing meeting, namely that everything which ought to have been done has been done and there are no predictable obstacles to what is to be done in the next period.

I suggest that you adopt a simple agenda something like the following:

- ✔ Activities accomplished since last progress report.
- ✔ Problems, if any, which have been encountered in accomplishing these activities.
- ✔ Information, data or feelings which have emerged while completing the activities.
- ✔ Activities to be accomplished before the next meeting.
- ✔ Potential problems, if any, in accomplishing these activities on time.
- ✔ Suggestions about what may be done, either by the client or the consultant, to speed up the process without loss of quality.
- ✔ The client's satisfaction or otherwise so far. (Delight is a better, though overused and devalued, word for how you ought to be left feeling at the end of each discussion.)

The purpose of the progress briefing is to provide you with the following benefits:

- ❑ You are assured of being completely abreast of progress and you are able, on the basis of your priorities, to redirect the consultant if the need arises. Sometimes there is limited day-to-day contact between consultant and client. Where this is the case, you may, without interfering with the consultant's ability to get the job done, choose to hold more frequent meetings. These can of course be at any time of day, within reason, to fit your no doubt busy schedule. I rarely object to having a client buy me a drink in the evening or breakfast in the morning if it improves our communication and our relationship.
- ❑ You gain and keep control over the project.

- ❑ You have better and more timely information when you have to report to your bosses, possibly including major shareholders.
- ❑ Regular involvement means that you have a better understanding of the value of what is being done in your name and your satisfaction is increased by pride in that achievement.
- ❑ Reporting regularly and in detail, possibly even in writing if yours is that kind of organization, forces the consultant to focus on what is really important.
- ❑ You know if difficulties are likely to arise. You or your consultant can take action to avoid what is avoidable and can develop contingency plans in good time to be ready for what may otherwise take you by surprise.

Written reports

Some consultants love to write reports. They are very good at it and the work of a couple of hours can easily be made to look like the output of several days.

A client of mine used one of the major consultancies. The result of their labors was a report of immense proportions and an invoice for $80,000. Impressive as it was, the report was also, if not unreadable, not easily read by busy executives. The client therefore asked if it would be possible to distill the findings into a shorter document. This arrived with pleasing alacrity and a further invoice for $18,000. Finding little in the report which seemed to him to be relevant, the client showed it to me.

I told him that it is not my place to evaluate a fellow professional's work, but he insisted that I take it away and read it, even though I would not be prepared to comment on it subse-

Maximizing the Benefit

quently. Since I was to carry out some consultancy work for which the report might have been relevant, I read it. It was pure desk research which I am confident a competent journalist could have put together in a day, or a green bean of moderate intelligence could easily have compiled in two. A total of close on $100,000 for what, in quality terms, was at most three days' work is good business.

As a client, however, you may need interim reports. These may, for example, form the basis for procedural guides and references through and after the project. You may want them as a record which targets and specifies problems. You may want them because you are more comfortable with the written word. You may, and I say this without personal criticism, want them because you work in an organization where it is wise to cover your backside. Whatever your reason, remember that you are paying for them. So it is wise to insist on reports which are brief, to the point and readable.

You may wish to require that the report:

- ✔ Presents quantified data on progress in terms of the percentage of the project completed by measuring work done and then comparing that with time and money spent.
- ✔ Concentrates on outcomes achieved, not events experienced.
- ✔ Avoids consultant speak so that it is immediately understood by anyone who needs to read it now and in the future.
- ✔ Uses visual aids not to pretty things up, but to save reading time.
- ✔ Reports only on facts and data supported by facts. No claims, no hyperbole, no consultant aggrandizement, just facts.
- ✔ Is completed and delivered on time. If you have a serious reason for needing a report you will almost certainly need it to be timely.

The client's responsibilities

When you are spending relatively large sums of your organization's money, it is important that your management of the initiative facilitates rather than hinders success. This means that your responsibilities are as much to the consultant as they are to the corporation. You must provide the following:

Phased payments to the agreed schedule. There are few things in business life which distract from the job in hand more than not receiving money when it is expected. An old colleague in GM was aware of this and moved heaven, earth and the chairman of the board to ensure that his team got what was coming to them when they expected it. If you have similarly to move sun and moon to get the finance department to act, please do it. It will make a difference worth far more than the illusory joy felt by the devoted bean counter when hanging on to a check.

A supportive environment. While the consultant is in your organization she is part of your team. Just as you ensure that your subordinates are able to do their work unfettered by interference and inappropriate consequences, please give the same benefit to your consultant. Her output will justify your effort.

Timely and relevant feedback. It is a feature of human behavior that not only does what is rewarded, intentionally or otherwise, get done, but what is not corrected is assumed to be correct. If you suspect that your consultant is going off course, tell her straight and tell her soon. If it turns out that you simply don't understand what is happening she will put you right, but if she is going off track you are paying, possibly in more ways than one, for her diversion. Don't let embarrassment stop you from getting her back on the correct path at the earliest possible moment.

Other considerations

These are so self-evident that they are little more than a shopping list. In the interest of completeness, however, I jot them down as factors of which you ought to be in control.

Confidentiality. No worthwhile professional would breach confidentiality in any way, but neither would any good consultant object to signing a confidentiality agreement. If you feel that a formal agreement is advisable, it is your business and your decision.

Conflicts of interest. If you are in the widget business and you believe that you must only be served by consultants who do not work for other widget makers, you are probably unwise but that is your right. Some years ago Ford Motor Company in the UK had a policy of only using consultancies who were prepared to undertake to do no work for other automotive manufacturers. As a consultant who, at that time, concentrated mainly on the motor business I had to convince them that it was precisely my knowledge of their sector which would be the source of added value and that, although I know of no way to unlearn what I knew, I would never breach their trust. They gave me the job, but the right to decide for themselves what might constitute a conflict of interest remained theirs, as it does yours.

Rights to outcomes. If you ask me to design a training program for your executives which you want to keep to yourselves, I will charge you for the time spent on design and development. If you want me to design a program which has general applicability and which I am free to offer to others as I choose, I will charge you considerably less. My contract will make this clear, but where the contract does not specify the ownership of outcomes, you should do so, in writing.

The use of subcontractors or associates. You should specify, where the contract does not, the procedure for bringing other consultants into your business. At the very least you should insist that no one comes on to your premises without your running the rule over them and approving them. A little more attention to this might keep some of the green beans at bay.

Transferability of the contract. The circumstances under which you, the client, can dismiss the consultant and transfer the contract to another should be fully understood. If I have my way such circumstances are limited to:

- the death of the consultant
- gross incompetence of the consultant (not likely if you do your job properly).

Conversely, the consultant should fire the client, and lose her income, if:

- it becomes clear that they cannot work effectively together
- her account is unpaid
- the assignment becomes too complex or too difficult for

her to execute to the highest possible professional standards.

Abnormal expense. The consultant should be free to claim normal expenses without prior authority, but what is to constitute abnormal expense and how it is to be authorized needs to be clear.

Time management. Within the limits of what is appropriate to a professional adviser, you have the right to insist that time is properly accounted for. Since the client pays for everything you will pay for the time spent accounting for time, so good sense as well as good taste suggest that the accounting should not be too onerous.

Non-performance. If you have the right consultant this will not happen, but just in case you may wish to specify what constitutes non-performance − for example deadlines missed, outcomes not achieved, fomenting a strike.

How to get consultancy without paying

These ideas will not work with a good consultant such as those I have trained, but there are people out there whose naivety makes them, certainly not fair, but easy game.

Badly written proposals are a simple source of free consultancy. Anxious to impress, the consultant writes down exactly how, step by step, she intends to solve your problem. With a recipe rather than a proposal, all that remains for you to do is to assess the credibility of the method and then do the easy bit, either using internal resources or another, possibly cheaper, consultant.

It is never good for the client to depend on the consultant. It gets worse when, in an effort to give superlative service, the consultant is happy to make 'follow-up' visits without charge. It is easy, even when you have a good consultant, to take advantage of her desire to offer superb aftersales service. This starts with 'You know old Fred, he never manages to grasp things the first dozen times they are explained. Could you just pop by and go through it with him again?' and moves to 'I've had a wonderful idea. Could you just call in and let me bounce it off you?' You could end up with free consultancy for life. Few of us are comfortable telling the client that added value and customer service have their limits.

Sometimes the wily client invites the consultant to show what she can do by giving a free diagnosis of the problem. Einstein was right when he said that any damned fool can come up with the answer if a genius asks the right question. If she diagnoses your problem without charge she has done the difficult part and there is little reason, in spite of your protestations to the contrary, to give her a worthwhile contract to come up with and implement the solution.

I train consultants to respond by pointing out that they are professionals who always get paid for what they do. Alternatively, if they think that the competition will naively fall for your wiles, they will say: 'I will diagnose your problem for you, charging you my usual daily rate. If subsequent to my diagnosis you give me a contract worth not less than $X000 to arrive at and implement a solution, I will cancel that invoice. Otherwise I will expect immediate payment.' If that sounds hard to you, please write and tell me when someone last prospered in business by being a fool.

With the unwary you can extend the above into having the whole job done without charge by promising the earth – next time. Of course, next time never comes. When people come to me for advice on how to start and build their business I ask how they propose to market themselves. More than a few tell me that they intend to offer their services free to show what they can do and then pick up huge and highly profitable contracts. The ways of the world are such that I have to remind them of Sam Goldwyn's dictum that not only is a verbal agreement not worth the paper it is written on, but a service, given free of charge, is not regarded as being worth what was paid for it.

A diversion can work wonders. Suppose that you have a number of divisions and an excellent consultant working at one of them. She is performing near miracles and you realize that much good could come from her spending a little time at Plant A (for awful) where they have similar problems. You accost her thus: 'You're doing a wonderful job and I really appreciate your skills and your effort. Could you do me the greatest of personal favors and just pop over to Plant A and quickly put them right?' Using the terms 'personal favor' and 'quickly' contributes a note of ambiguity which beguiles the fair. It only appears to be a small job and she is doing it for you. Will she charge you, her esteemed client, for the opportunity to provide a little added value? Most will not.

Those whom I have trained, however, will smile their sweetest smile and reply:

> 'How kind of you to notice how well things are going. I am so grateful. Certainly I will be happy to go and look at things in Plant A for you. Since I have to get this plant completed by 30 March and that means a tight timetable, I will put it into my diary for 1 April. If you need me to go before that would you give me a brief note to that effect. I realize that my performance is being judged on what I achieve at this plant, and if the timetable is thrown out of sync I wouldn't want people to think it is because I am inefficient. And while we are talking of putting things in writing, I will give you an amendment to my original

proposal so that you have as little trouble as possible when you seek authorization for the additional expenditure.'

Of course there are thousands of consultants whom I have yet to train and they may be deemed to deserve all that they get if they do not show the same judgment.

Training the internal consultancy team

Presumably the people in an internal consultancy team were chosen because they showed aptitude and because they had technical skills which are valued widely in the organization. That is an excellent start and many consultants in the commercial field go no further. That is, in part, why there are so many substandard consultants out there.

If you have gone to the trouble of establishing an internal consultancy team, you will want to kickstart the process by considering what training would be useful early on. Based on successfully training a substantial number of external and internal consultants, the following would seem to be the minimum required:

- An advanced introduction to consultancy which covers the profession in sufficient detail to ensure that newcomers understand the ethics of the business and can build their own status and reputation, plan an intervention, write a proposal and identify opportunities, attract business, manage the intervention and so on.
- Consultancy tools and techniques.
- Selling the service and solution to the client.
- Understanding and managing human behavior.
- Creative and rational problem-solving techniques.

Maximizing the Benefit

❑ Understanding the business organization and how functions interact in unexpected ways.

Training must be interactive and practical, dealing with the specific real world which the consultant will encounter. It should also be designed and conducted so that learning and the transfer of that learning are optimized (how to do this is discussed in Chapter 13). Making this effort will ensure that you make the best of the capabilities of your internal team.

13

Making Training Work

The difference between the wise and clever man is that the clever man can extricate himself from a situation into which the wise man would not have got in the first place.

Jewish aphorism

TRAINING IS AN ESSENTIAL PART OF ALL CONSULTANCY ASSIGNments and consultants are usually delighted to provide it. However, training often fails to work. Why is this the case?

It starts at the University of Columbia where an expert, Bruce Joyce, began a global research program into the effectiveness of training. He found that the actual transfer and use of what is taught in the workplace were, to put it mildly, disappointing. For example, if your favorite internal or external trainer, Motormouth Magee, gives a series of traditional 'chalk and talk' lectures, the sum total of his divulged knowledge taken away and used by participants is less than 5 percent.

Aha, you are thinking, our trainers are more modern than that. Modish MacGrew offers only the best in experiential training. Well, training delivered by Modish will be a little more effective, but only a little. The research suggests that when the method is experiential, either the participants learn nothing because they reject what they see as silly games, or the level of transfer to the workplace goes up to around 5 percent rather than the somewhat less than 5 percent that we experience with chalk and talk.

Can we improve the levels of understanding and use through traditional methods? If we teach skills and have people practice them in a truly threat-free environment, the results are better. The level of transfer to the workplace is between 10 and 15 percent. Still a poor return on your investment, but is it better? Not really. A separate study by the Xerox Corporation found that 87 percent of what is learned and transferred is lost within 12 weeks unless special steps are taken to reinforce the learning. I think you will agree that, on the face of it, 13 percent of 15 percent (1.95 percent) of anything rarely justifies the investment, so what can be done?

If information has to be put across to a large number of people in a relatively short time, the best approach is still the training program or workshop, but it must be designed to be effective. That means that the vast majority of consultants and trainers, internal and external, need to rethink the way they approach the development process. It is not a matter of methodology. Although practical real-world workshops work best, they are far from ideal unless the whole operation is designed from the ground up to be effective.

Sustained transfer of learning

To ensure and sustain effective transfer of learning, the following must apply:

- ✔ Management must own and want the training. They must understand that the training will solve a problem or enable an activity which is important to them and justifies their active participation in making it work.

- ✔ The objectives of the training must be expressed as specific recognizable behaviors which all participants will exercise after the training has taken place. It is essential to note two things here:
  - The behaviors must be possible for all attendees to perform and relevant to achieving the outcome that management are seeking.
  - The objectives must say that all participants *will* perform those behaviors after training and not be couched in the trainer's preferred universal get-out of 'will be able to'. Unless people do what they have been trained to do nothing has been gained by training them other creating a temporary sense of warmth and comfort.

- ✔ Management, as the owners of the program, must be trained sufficiently to be able to act as coaches, mentors and informed supporters.

- ✔ The program must be sufficiently long to achieve the objectives, but not necessarily immediately because

- ✔ people should preferably attend in self-selected pairs who will coach each other and share their knowledge and skills after the program.

- ✔ A brief session, supported by carefully designed checklists, will be integrated into every program, teaching peer coaching skills.

- ✔ Formal peer coaching periods of, say, 10 minutes a day must be timetabled so that timely and regular coaching takes place which focuses on selected skills and actual behaviors.

- ✔ Managers and supervisors support peer coaching by recognizing effective use of what has been taught and, where practical, acting as role models of the desired behaviors.

- ✔ Behavioral checklists fully reflecting the objectives must be part of the seminar documentation. These checklists must be available to everyone and must clearly describe recognizable and demonstrable behaviors.

- ✔ Managers and participants should be made aware that there is an unavoidable 'learning dip' which takes place when we are integrating what we have learned and should know how to recognize and handle this blip in our development of new skills and applied knowledge.

- ✔ Those who have already experienced the training should, where practicable, brief their colleagues who will attend subsequently on what they will be expected to do after training and how they will be helped to achieve it.

Seward and Gers conducted a 12-year longitudinal study which shows that, if what is described above is done properly, the transfer to the workplace of what has been taught can be raised to 96 percent and kept there or improved. In my own practice it was this game plan explained to a training team in a single day which enabled them to design and conduct training leading to a 180 percent increase in sales revenues in three months.

A quick, rule-of-thumb judgment of just how much more autonomous, self-reliant and capable your people will be after an intervention might be to ask your consultant or trainer, internal or external, to tell you about Seward and Gers, or Bruce Joyce. If they are able to do so, ask how they intend to ensure that your people are taught in such a way that they will be able, without external reference, to handle all such situations in the future.

Achieving extraordinary results from workshops

One of the quickest ways of developing extraordinary levels of commitment and achievement is through well-facilitated workshops with the people who will be ultimately the key to making it all happen. However, workshop facilitation is not a skill which everyone possesses.

At the beginning of any relatively unstructured group workshop, mistrust and misunderstanding may well be high. Some of the participants will have been through what they will see as the same exercise before. If that workshop descended into a mere talking shop their negativism will far exceed their hopes, although they may be far too polite to show it.

It is essential, therefore, that the consultant has the group identify what outcomes would be a proper use of their time and commit herself entirely to their attainment. If the situation which led to the workshop is unclear to the group, she may need to position them on why they are there and what the organization is hoping to get from them before they will be able to clarify the outcomes.

It is also essential that the facilitator clarifies her role. She must explain that she is not a subject expert and not a school monitor. She is there with the sole purpose of helping the group achieve an outcome that they will be proud of in the time they have available.

Warming up

Many excellent facilitators, and many participants, like to have warm-up exercises at the beginning of a workshop. While I am not against these, I prefer to keep short workshops – one day or less – businesslike and focused on the outcome. I am concerned that nothing done is in any way perceived as wasting time or playing games.

My preferred first participant activity is to have each person complete a large sheet of flipchart paper on which they write:

❏ their name
❏ what experience, skills and knowledge they have which will be useful to the team in moving us to our goal
❏ what special contribution they will make to achieving our purpose.

These sheets will be on display throughout the workshop. Once people are clearly comfortable with the task and the situation, I will ask each person to read their sheet, add to it should they wish to do so and sign it. If the circumstances allow a Polaroid shot of each participant will be attached to their sheet.

The purpose of the public statement of intent, the signature and the ongoing identification with their commitment through the photograph is psychological and may be perceived by some readers as a little underhand. Research shows that what people publicly commit to they tend to carry through in the face of all difficulties. This small activity almost guarantees the success of the workshop.

Issues and concerns

It is essential, early in any workshop, to bring out participants' issues and concerns. It is equally important to ensure that this does not degenerate into a bull session in which nothing is gained other than the swapping of war stories and the sharing of frequently aired grievances. To avoid this I like to use an idea which I borrowed, stole might be a better word, from Federal Express. All concerns are raised in the form of problems to be solved: 'How are we going to...?' All concerns are captured on flipchart paper, and those that the group agree will seriously affect our ability to achieve our objective are taken to a separate room by a small sub-group which works on solutions. (The number of such problems is usually very small, one or two at most.)

If any solution makes sense to the whole group, is seen by them as essential and requires senior management approval, I invite the appropriate senior manager to join us and have the group put to her their concern and their solution. My experience is either that the preferred solution is 'signed off' on the spot, or that the executive commits to coming back with a feasible solution and the work continues without further looking back over the shoulder at old annoyances. These visits by senior managers are normally arranged for coffee, lunch or tea breaks, so little if any working time is lost.

Facilitation

Social psychology research has established that the optimal group size is five. If a group is of six or more, at least one person will be frozen out of any discussion. Therefore subgroups should not exceed five people.

When the whole group is in plenary session a key responsibility of the facilitator is to ensure that each person has an opportunity to express their opinions and ideas without putting uncomfortable pressure on the quieter ones. I often find that I have to silence the archetypal group member who only lets someone say two words before jumping in with: 'What Tom is really trying to say is...' After a while, if handled gently, any such interruption becomes a group in-joke and no one is hurt.

Depending on the confidence and education of group members, the facilitator may need to offer some tips on conversational skills. This is particularly likely when participants come from several functions and a wide spread of hierarchical levels. Recognizing each other's valued contribution without such recognition becoming a formula, listening for cues such as the voice trailing off when the speaker wants someone else to take over, using open and closed questions, giving an accurate and empathetic summary of what has been said – all of these can be learned, if needed, in minutes. The facilitator should be ready to explain and demonstrate each, but only in direct response to actual problems emerging within the group. It is not her role to predetermine what must be taught, but to be prepared for what might be necessary.

All the important points which emerge should be made visible. This often means that the facilitator abridges what has been said, writing a note on to a flipchart. Because it usually reads well the note is seldom challenged, but often a key thought has been lost in translation. Where possible the facilitator should have the groups do their own recording so that they recognize what is written as their own.

During plenary sessions have people write their comments with bold felt-tip pens on to cards which can be pinned or Blu-tacked to a surface. If facilities exist to photograph all cards in situ, photocopy and distribute the results so that each individual can recognize their own contribution and be confident that nothing has been changed by the facilitator. Not only does this offer a more reliable record of the group's output, it can be left in place for other groups to add to – and it reduces talking as people concentrate on writing their ideas legibly and quickly.

A good facilitator will be armed with small stickers which can be attached by group members to a predrawn 'opinionnaire' to create an instant histogram of their feelings. This small technique can be used to create openness in a highly charged situation. People are asked to decide where on a Likert scale their choice would be and they rush up together to place their stickers with the minimum of individual visibility and the maximum of energy.

For example:

In this organization morale at present is:
0 – marginally better than in death row
1 – low
2 – a little worse than we would like it to be
3 – average for a business
4 – good
5 – wonderful

It is even more illuminating to have a different colored sticker which can be placed to show another dimension:

and it is:
0 – getting worse every day
1 – in a slow decline
2 – becoming neither worse nor better
3 – getting better
4 – improving at an unbelievable rate
5 – going into orbit

A small but significant point: a skilled facilitator will never produce a scale with an odd number of points. The middle point is too attractive an alibi for those who like to sit firmly on the fence. An even number ensures that each person is forced to take a position on one side of the divide. This is far more likely to get people sharing ideas than is the undivided middle.

The facilitator should identify and emphasize those outputs of discussion which imply action. The success of a workshop is in direct proportion to the effective actions which are implemented afterwards. The facilitator can do this without appearing to take a controlling role by asking questions such as:

- 'Is this something you would want to take some kind of action about?'
- 'Should we highlight this so you can find it easily when you are putting together your action plan?'

All decisions should appear to remain with the group, although it is a poor facilitator who fails to give direction or support when it would help the group achieve high-quality outcomes.

There is, of course, more to facilitation. The good facilitator has many tools at her disposal and knows, above all, when *not* to use one of them. She can balance sometimes conflicting needs so that, although she shows great sensitivity to the needs of individuals, she is never deflected from the purpose of the activity. She uses her sensitivity, her people and process skills to only one end: high value outcomes.

Afterword

To be successful you have to be lucky, or a little mad, or very talented, or find yourself in a rapid growth field.
                                        Edward de Bono

I WROTE THIS BOOK TO TRY TO MAKE A SMALL CONTRIBUTION TO ensuring that, in a world in which the need to use consultancy is growing all the time, outcomes would be of increasingly high quality and value to clients.

For the last two decades the volume of consultancy has increased at around 20 percent a year, every year. In 1997 it increased by 27 percent. It is a multibillion-dollar business. Peter Drucker's prediction that every manager would need consultancy support to keep abreast of what is happening in the rapidly changing business world has been proved true with a vengeance.

Consultancy can make, or sadly break, your business. What is more, you have it in your hands to ensure that when you choose to use consultants, external, internal or a combination, you demand and know how to get high value. If you get this right, the value can be high indeed.

As a final checklist, the main messages of this book can be summarized as follows:

- ❑ Define exactly what your problem is before you start looking for a consultant.
- ❑ Educate yourself about the kinds of consultants and consultancies that exist.
- ❑ Decide whether it might be to your organization's long-term benefit to develop an internal consultancy capability.
- ❑ If you decide to use external consultants, spend time, effort and imagination on finding precisely the right one(s) for you.
- ❑ Be aware that those who are the best at selling their services may not in fact be the best consultants.
- ❑ Be sure that you grasp in full what the consultant will be doing for you, when, in what way and how much it will cost.
- ❑ Insist on frequent progress briefings and use them to check that the intervention remains on track.
- ❑ Use the consultant and suitable activities to assist in the development of your own people's capabilities.
- ❑ Know how to maximize the benefit from the process at each stage.

There are many excellent and some quite brilliant consultants out there. I hope this book will enable you to find them. Keep looking, because whatever else you do, you are almost certain to need them one day.

Bibliography

IN MY EXPERIENCE, BUSY EXECUTIVES BUY MORE BOOKS THAN THEY have time to read. Rather than add to a rapidly growing library of less than useful buys, I list here a few carefully selected books and try to explain why I believe you ought to read them.

Ashford, Martin (1998) *Con Tricks*, **Simon & Schuster**
A book by a former consultant with Deloitte & Touche on what the big name consultancies are like to work for and with.

Crainer, Stuart (1996) *Key Management Ideas*, **Pitman**
By far the most useful and comprehensive book concerning the ideas which have created modern management. Anyone who takes the possibility of 'doing it themselves' seriously ought to have this book available and insist that all internal consultants and trainers read, learn and inwardly digest, as they used to say in my far-off school days. It is worth a bundle of MBAs.

Furnham, Adrian (1996) *All in the Mind*, **Whurr**
Psychology, that is pop psychology, has become the eternal fad and, as a result, fallacies and futilities abound. In this short and clear book, Adrian explains what we really know about human behavior at work and elsewhere. Intelligent reading will enable the consultant and the client to avoid being one of the 70 percent of failures of the business process reengineering disaster or the 90+ percent of empowerment disasters.

Geneen, Harold and Bowers, Brent (1997) *The Synergy Myth*, **St Martins Press**
If Peter Drucker is the doyen of business thinkers, Geneen is certainly the grand old man of consultancy. In this book he explodes the myths of downsizing, reengineering, culture change and the rest, but more importantly he tells the reader exactly what to do to put business back on the straight and narrow path to prosperity.

de Geus, Arie (1997) *The Living Company*, **Nicholas Brealey**
Arie has studied businesses which are long-term survivors at a time when attrition is accelerating. This important book contains the fruits of that research. It explains why some businesses survive for hundreds of years while others go into decline and die in a decade or less. What is more, it tells you how to be one of the winners. This book might as easily have been called 'The Learning Company' and that is what consultancy, internal or bought-in, is all about.

Gilley, Jerry and Eggland, Steven (1992) *Marketing HRD within Organizations*, Jossey-Bass
A useful book which provides a blueprint for marketing training and development – by extension, consultancy inside the organization.

Lambert, Tom (1996) *The Power of Influence*, Nicholas Brealey
Modesty forbids, so let me quote Richard Donkin of the *Financial Times*: '[There is a] repertoire of professional influencing skills covered in Lambert's book which makes some of the more interesting psychological observations in the field accessible.'

Lambert, Tom (1996) *Key Management Solutions*, Pitman
Equally useful as a management or a consultancy toolkit.

Lambert, Tom (1997) *High Income Consulting*, 2nd edn, Nicholas Brealey
What the most successful consultants in the world actually do to sustain their success.

Lambert, Tom (1997) *Making Change Pay*, Financial Times
A step-by-step toolkit for successful organizational change.

Margerison, Charles (1988) *Managerial Consulting Skills*, **Gower**
The first and the best primer for the internal consultant. Explains group facilitation skills in detail by focusing on what Margerison does with client groups. A masterclass between hard covers.

McGuinness, Kevin and Short, Tom (1997) *Using the Net for Research in Business and Law*, **Old Bailey Press**
If you need to do research this book is an essential; if you surf the Net in order to learn, it is also a delightful guide to the best sources of information.

Micklethwait, John and Wooldridge, Adrian (1996) *The Witch Doctors*, **Heinemann**
A careful and balanced analysis of the work of the big name consultants by two journalists from the *Economist*. A book which is as readable as it is instructive.

O'Shea, James and Madigan, Charles (1997) *Dangerous Company*, **Times Business (USA)/Nicholas Brealey (UK)**
A detailed analysis by investigative journalists into the triumphs and disasters of the consulting business. This book provided the information on which I analysed the Figgie calamity and, sensitivities being what they are, it is the book about which a great deal of fuss has been made. If you want to be 'in the swim' you cannot afford to be the one person in your circle who has not read this.

Schaffer, Robert (1997) *High Impact Consulting*, Jossey-Bass
Schaffer has some interesting ideas on how to turn the short-term success of consulting initiatives into long-term client gains and his book will be of interest to clients of outside consultants and internal teams alike.

Trompenaars, Fons and Hampden-Turner, Charles (1997) *Riding the Waves of Culture*, **2nd edn, Nicholas Brealey**
Using research involving 30,000 employees in 50 countries, Trompenaars shows why misunderstandings are rife among different national cultures even when part of the same firm. An essential reference book for those working globally, whether consultant or executive.

Index

A

accountancy firms 7
accreditation 44, 77
advisory consultants 25–6, 128
advocate role 31–2
articles, writing 162–3

B

behavior, influencing 17–18
benefits 108–109
big firms 5–8, 37–8, 130
   advantages of 37–8
   disadvantages of 38
books, writing 163–4

C

candidates
   evaluating 102–104
   identifying 98–101

clients
   responsibilities of 80
   what they do wrong 10
   what they need 9–10
collaborator role 34–5
colleges and universities 101
confidentiality 179
conflict of interest 179
consensus 52–3
consultancy
   free 181–4
   growth of 4–10
   when it goes wrong x
consultants
   benefits of using x–xi
   categorizing 23–44
   duties of 80
   effective 13–14
   finding the right one 97–113
   inexperienced 6–7; see also green beans
   previously used 98–9, 122–4
   relationship with clients 5

consultants (*cont.*)
  requirements of 3–4,
    102–103
  why organizations need
    4–5, 47–61
consulting intervention
  150–54
consulting process 147–55
contract, sample 139–42
contracts 137–43, 149
  purposes of 137
  written by lawyers 138
costs, controlling x, 16,
  83–4
customers, profitable 56–9

D

de Geus, Arie 49, 51
declining business, consultants 111–12
divergent thinking 30
dominance strategy 49–50,
  52, 53
Drucker, Peter 48, 52–3, 56,
  127, 197

E

educator role 33–4
expert role 31, 32–3
experts 70–71

external consultants 13, 63,
  64–6, 147–8, 158
  advantages of 64, 65
  disadvantages of 64, 65

F

facilitation 191, 193–6
fact finder role 36–7
fees 109–10, 125–31
  setting 127–31
Figgie International 81–93
flow chart of activities
  106–107, 173
Ford Motor Co 179
functional consultants
  28–30
functional specialists 28–30

G

Gantt charts 109, 173
General Electric 41
General Motors 71
Gers 72, 190
goals 48, 87
government intervention
  43–4
government organizations
  100
green beans 6–7, 76, 109
growth 52–6

H

Hamel, Gary 49
Harvey-Jones, Sir John 25–6, 126
High Income Consulting ix

I

identifier of alternatives role 35–6
industry expertise 28, 75
ineffective consultants, unmasking 70–78
information, sources of 100–101
internal consultancy team, announcing 156–61
internal consultants 13–21, 64, 65, 148
 advantages of 15–16, 65–6
 development of 17
 disadvantages of 66
 finding 19–20
 job satisfaction 16–18
 training 184–5

J

jargon 73–4
Joyce, Bruce 187, 188

K

Key Management Solutions ix, 147
knowledge 36–7, 53

L

Lambert's law 48
learning communities 51
learning, transfer of 187–90

M

Madigan, Charles 79–80, 92
managers, as fad junkies 5
manufacturing, world-class 54–6
marketing 148, 157–61
meetings, attending 158–60

N

name dropping 74–5
need analysis 60
newsletters 163
Nonaka 36, 53

O

O'Shea, James 79–80, 92
one-person consultancy firms
   7–9, 42–4
operational consultants
   24–5, 127–8
outcomes
   defining 60–61
   ownership of 180
overheads 129

P

payment 143–5
performance contracts 76,
   134–7
Peters, Tom 25–6, 126
Popcorn, Faith 25–6
power 33
Prahalad, Chris 49, 126
problems, defining 60–61
process consultants 27
professional associations
   100
progress briefings 165–6,
   174–6
proposals 106, 149, 168–73
public relations 148

Q

quality, improving 16

R

references 115–17
referrals 99–100, 118–21
registers of consultants 101
reports 176–7
responsibilities, of
   client 178–9
retainers 131–3
roles of consultants 30–37
roles, directive 31–4
roles, less directive 34–7

S

salespeople, consultants as
   30–31, 69
seminars 161–2
Seward 72, 190
small consultancy firms
   39–41
   advantages 39–40
   disadvantages 40–41
subcontractors 180
survival, of a business 49

T

Takeuchi 36, 53
Tamburrino, Liese 39
Tannen, Deborah 32–3
time, using productively 18
Townsend, Robert 90
trainer role 33–4
training, maximizing 187–96
transferability, of contract 180–81

W

workshops 191–6

X

Xerox Corp. 188